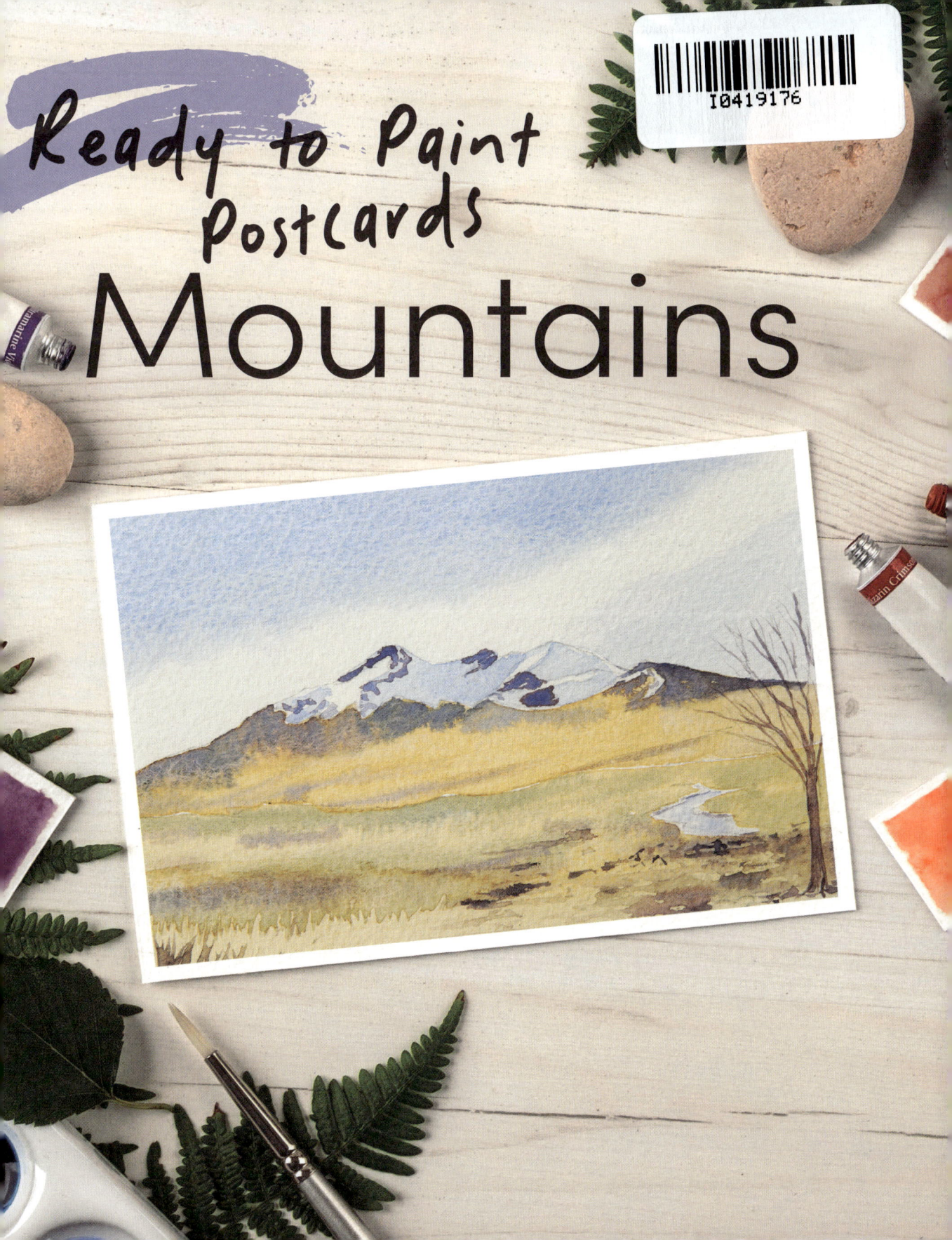

Ready to Paint
Postcards
Mountains

First published in 2026

Search Press Limited
Wellwood, North Farm Road,
Tunbridge Wells, Kent TN2 3DR

1 2 3 4 5 6 7 8 9 10

ISBN: 978-1-80092-296-9
ebook ISBN: 978-1-80093-287-6

Bookmarked Hub
Extra copies of the outlines are available to download free from the Bookmarked Hub. Search for this book by title or ISBN: the files can be found under 'Book Extras'. Membership of the Bookmarked online community is free: www.bookmarkedhub.com

Publishers' notes
The Publishers and author can accept no responsibility for any consequences arising from the information, advice or instructions given in this publication.

For errata, please visit our website (www.searchpress.com) or the Bookmarked Hub (www.bookmarkedhub.com).

GPSR information can be found
at www.searchpress.com
Printed in China, RRD112025

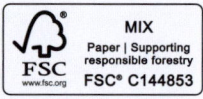

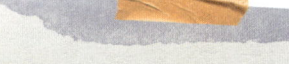

ACKNOWLEDGEMENTS

To my family, especially my parents and husband, and my friends who have all shared the ups and downs in the life of an artist. To my students and fellow painters who encourage and inspire; to Gavin Sawyer at Roddy Paine Photographic Studios for his patience, and to my ever-cheerful editor Edward Ralph and the lovely team at Search Press. Thanks also to St Cuthberts Mill for providing some of the paper used in preparing for this book.

Ready to Paint Postcards
Mountains

15 stunning watercolour paintings to
create in just 30 minutes

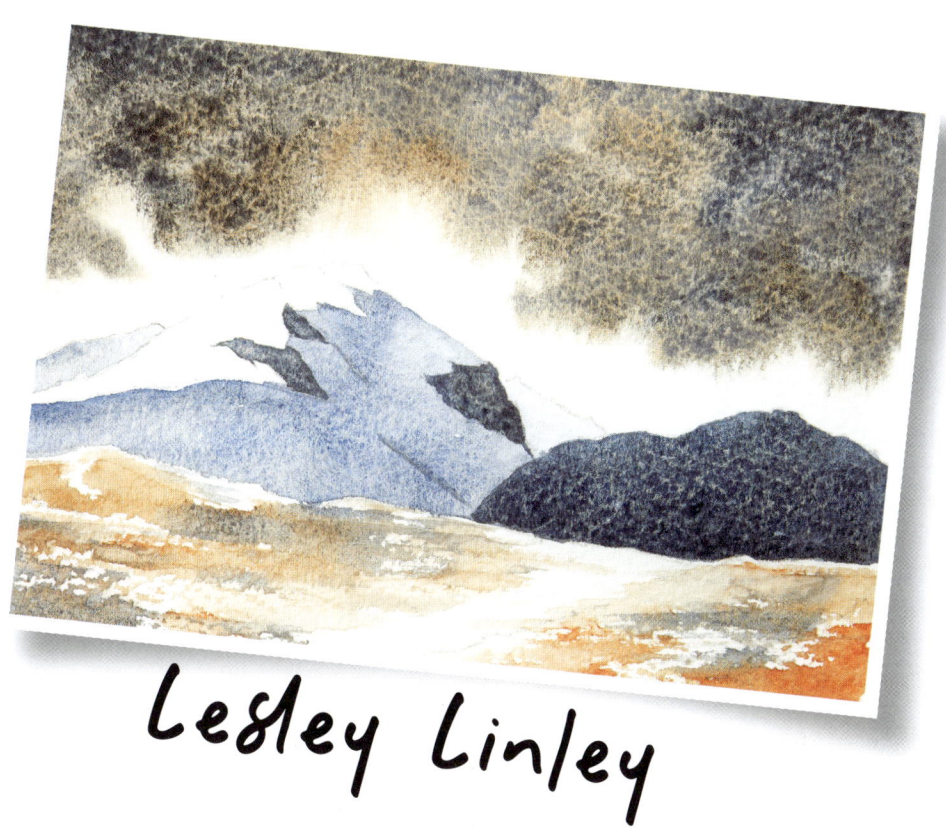

Lesley Linley

SEARCH PRESS

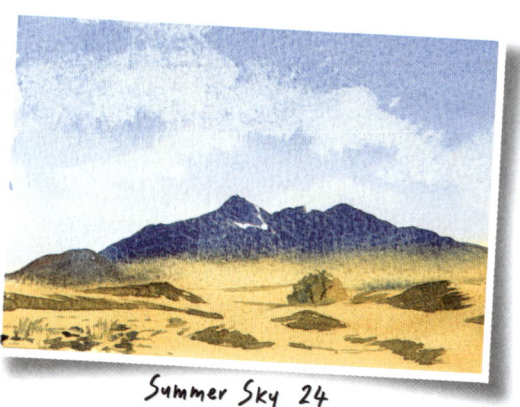
Summer Sky 24

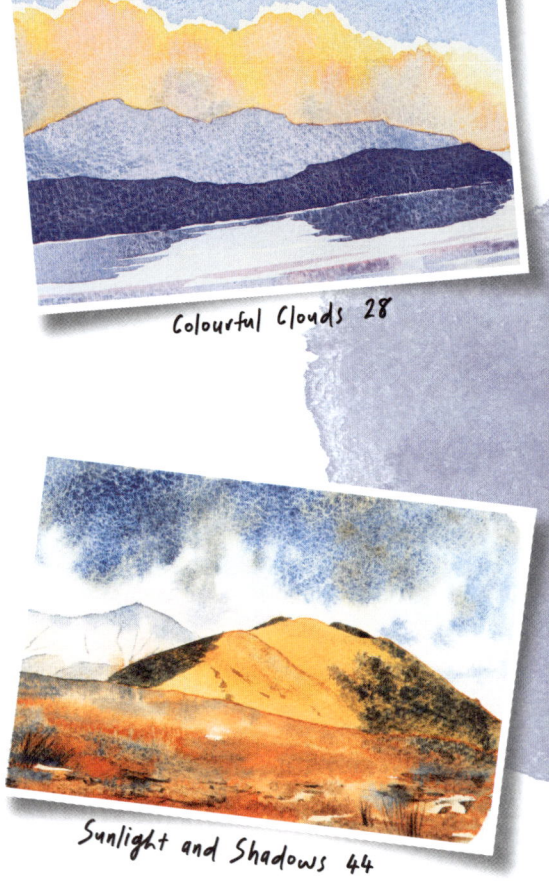
Colourful Clouds 28

Contents

Sunlight and Shadows 44

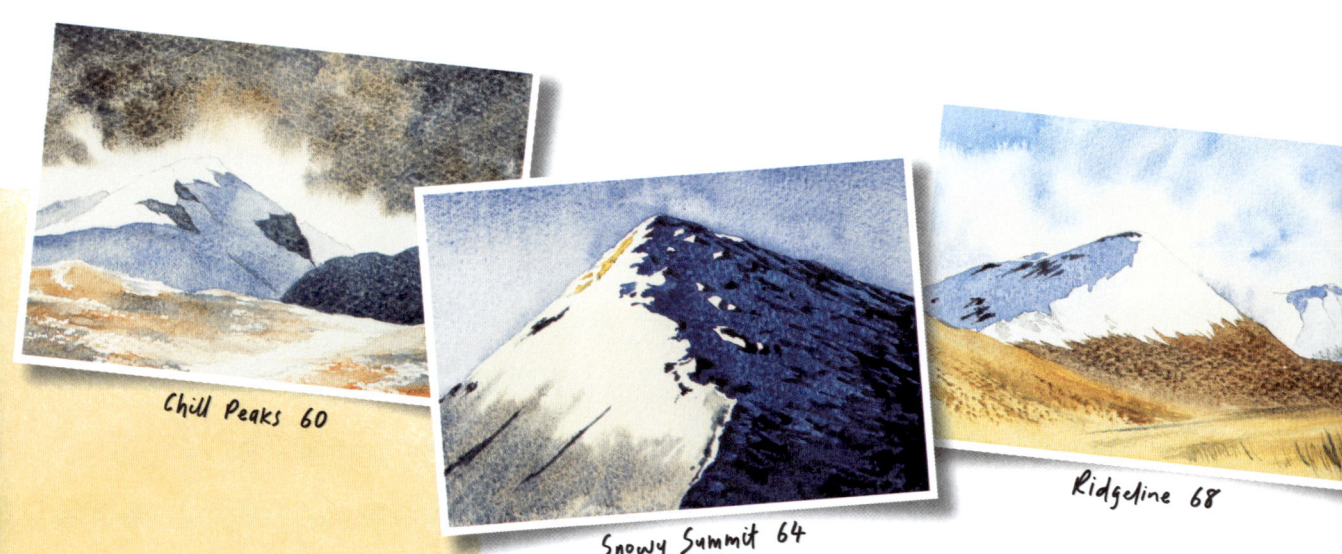
Chill Peaks 60

Snowy Summit 64

Ridgeline 68

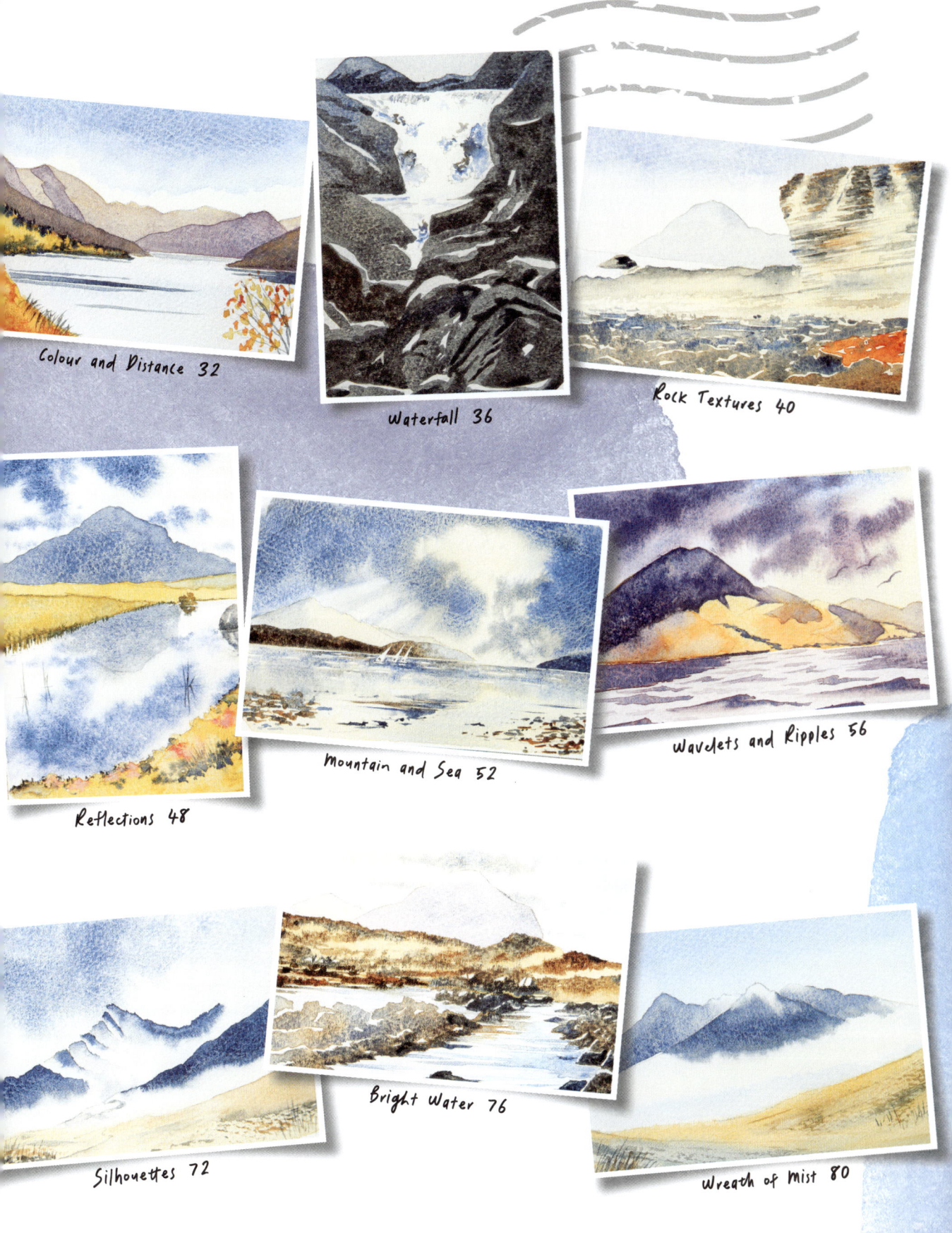

Introduction

I have always enjoyed teaching beginners; sharing their delight when they achieve beyond their expectations, turning 'I can't' into 'I did'. The thrill I get from that hasn't diminished over the years. I believe that anyone can learn if they are prepared to watch and listen (or read) and practise, practise, practise.

These 15 x 10cm (6 x 4in) projects allow you to learn in bitesize pieces by producing small paintings. For the step-by-step exercises, read all the instructions for each postcard and have everything to hand before starting to paint. Unless told otherwise within the individual project text, allow each step to dry before beginning the next. The suggested 30-minute painting time for these projects, encourages you to stop before overworking your painting. There is often a freshness in practice pieces that is lost when we set out to produce a finished painting.

If your first attempt isn't too successful, you can try again – in fact, you will benefit from working through each project more than once. Perhaps revisit the book a few weeks or months after working through it. As you become more familiar with the processes, it will be easier to see how you can use them in your own paintings when you break away from the book to work on your own. At that stage, keep the book handy: it will offer reassurance if you're having a bad day. Even the most experienced painter will have one of those occasionally.

None of these postcard projects shows the only way, or the correct way, to paint. These are suggestions; methods that I've found work for me and for my students. Every artist has their own way of working, preferred method and choice of materials. Find out what suits you. If a method works for you, even if you've just invented it, it's not wrong – simply different. Eventually you'll learn what you like and, with that all-important practice, will find that you can select the techniques and materials you need to pursue your own style and subjects.

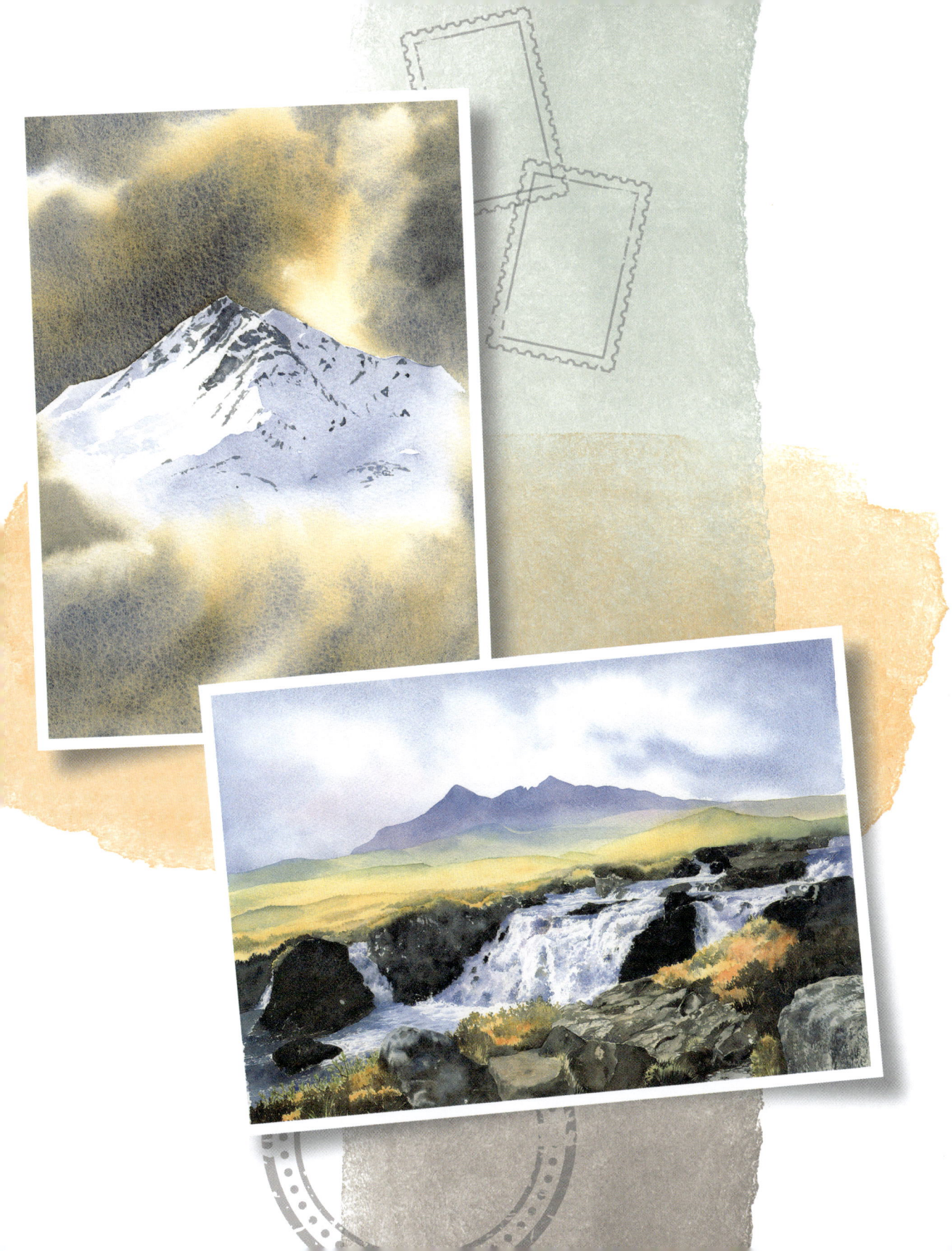

First steps with watercolour

This part of the book shows you how to get to grips with your materials – and have fun while you paint! Take a little time to get to grips with your tools and learn the fundamental painting techniques explained over the following pages. You'll then find additional techniques dotted throughout the book. By working through from the start, you'll find your skills build naturally as you go on.

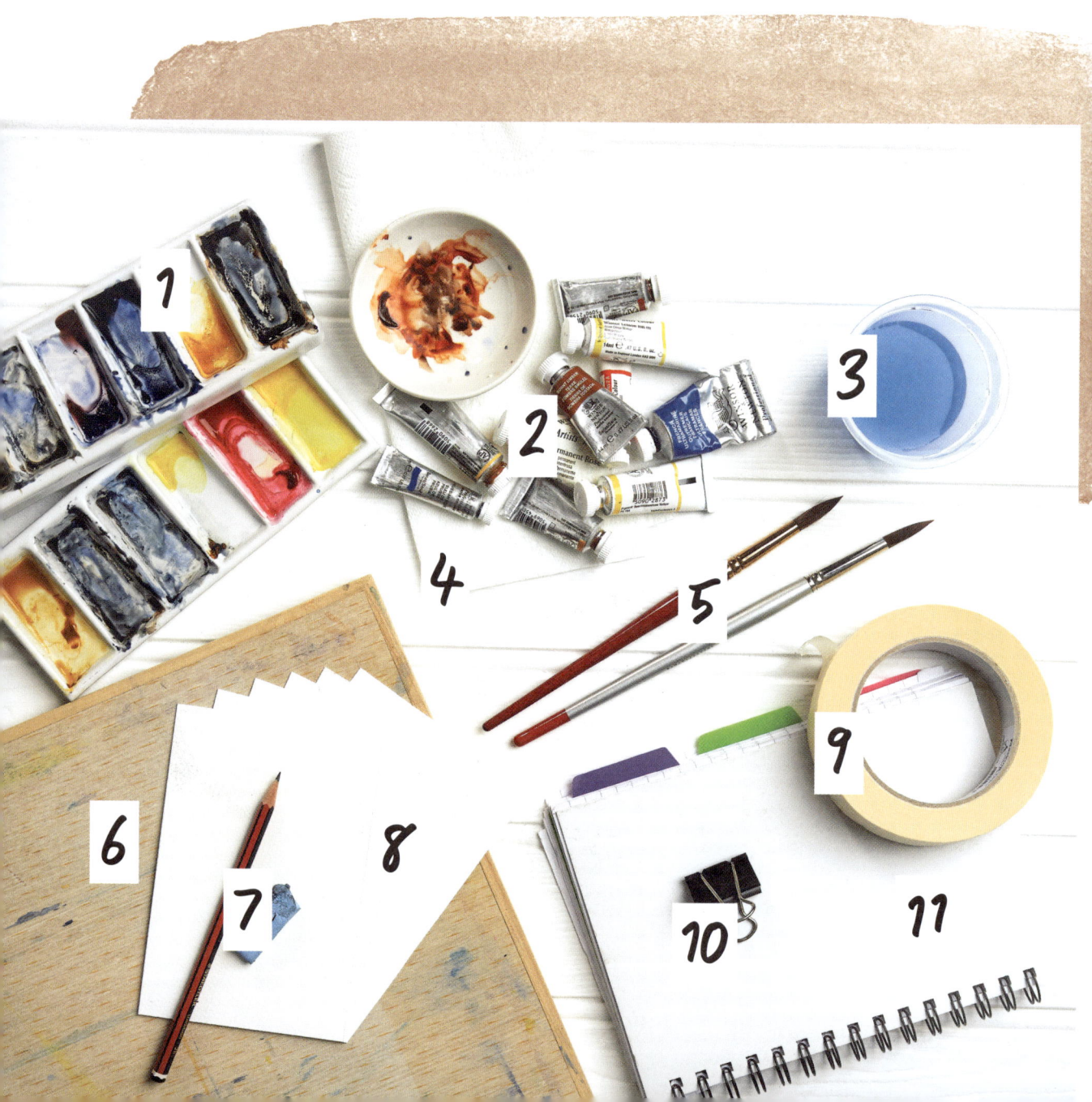

Basic painting equipment

1 Palette These are available in many sizes and types, in ceramic, plastic and metal. Small palettes and paint boxes rarely hold enough paint for a large wash so you may need extra containers for these. I use a ceramic palette (as it's easy to clean) with slanted wells for small quantities and a white plate for larger volumes of paint.

2 Paints A few well-chosen paints will suffice. Students' quality paints are an economical starting point, but try professional or artists' quality as soon as you can – you will use less, as the colours are stronger and more vibrant. Tubes can be easier to use when you need a large volume of colour, but for the small exercises in this book pans (solid blocks of paint that need to be wetted) are fine. You can also use a mixture of tubes and pans if you prefer.

3 Water pot It is helpful to have several water pots, one for clean water to dilute your paint, and one or more pots for rinsing brushes. A glass jar makes a useful water pot. Alternatively, you can use a plastic pot, which can be found in anti-spill versions.

4 Kitchen paper Useful for wiping brushes, lifting out paint, mopping up spills and cleaning palettes. Avoid coloured papers as the colour may bleed when lifting out (see page 25).

5 Brushes One good-quality size 10 round brush with a good point will do the job of many brushes, and is all you need for these projects. Buy the best you can afford: a high-quality brush made for watercolour painting from a reputable brand. Sable hair is expensive, but a good brush will last a long time if well looked after. The brush you choose should be comfortable to hold. Small brushes tend to have thin handles, larger brushes wider handles, and the length of handle can affect the balance in your hand.

6 Painting board A large, lightweight board is handy to lean upon, and will let you set your paper at an angle. This will help washes of paint to flow.

7 Pencil and eraser You will need a 2B pencil to transfer the outlines onto paper. Be careful to pencil lightly (the drawings shown in this book are intentionally heavier to help ensure you can see them). Scribble on scrap paper with a newly sharpened pencil to remove a too-sharp point so that you don't scratch the paper. I use a putty eraser for erasing pencil lines and removing surplus graphite from watercolour paper after tracing down.

8 Paper A 15 x 10cm (6 x 4in) pad or block of watercolour paper is ideal for the projects in this book, but you can also cut larger sheets down to size. Use good quality paper from a reputable manufacturer; find a paper you like and stick with it. Lightweight papers are cheaper than heavyweight, but will be more likely to cockle when wet. A good general-use paper is 300gsm (140lb) in weight, with a slightly textured surface known as Not or CP (Cold Pressed).

9 Masking tape If you wish to hold paper down on a board, this tape is useful – though if it's left on for long periods, it may leave a sticky residue. If you paint right up to the tape, leave your painting to dry before removing the tape or the paper may tear.

10 Metal clips These are a good alternative to masking tape for securing your paper to a board.

11 Notebook This will come in handy for recording your own notes. A well-maintained notebook will let you look back on what you tried and what happened. This is particularly handy when experimenting with colours and techniques.

Clean water is key

Change your rinsing water frequently; you won't get clear, fresh colours if you're not washing your brush properly.

Preparing your paint

The clue is in the name but isn't explained on the packaging: watercolour paint should be mixed (diluted) with water. It should flow when mixed and not need to be physically spread as you would when applying emulsion paint.

Watercolours become paler as they dry, so when preparing your paints you need to make your colours/tones stronger to allow for this.

Any paint left on your palette after a painting session can be used for practising brushstrokes, or warming up before beginning a painting.

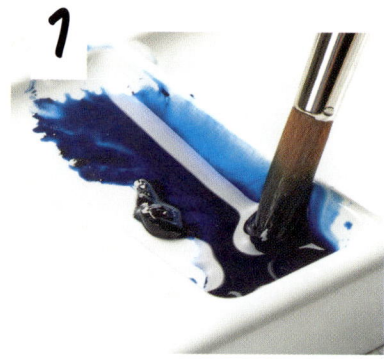

1

▶ Squeeze out a small amount of paint into a space on your palette. Wet a size 10 round brush and add water by gently brushing the brush over the paint.

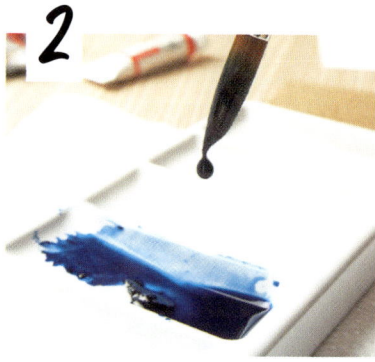

2

▶ Continue until the mix forms a drop which drips off your brush when held up as shown.

Brushstrokes

Before buying a large number of brushes, get to know what you can achieve with a single, good-quality size 10 round brush.

Simply playing with a brush will let you find out what can be achieved and is a relaxing introduction to watercolour. Improving your brush handling skills will certainly not be wasted time.

Fine lines Dampen your brush, load it in your prepared paint, then hold the brush upright and lightly draw the tip across the paper's surface. Avoid too much paint on your brush: a fully loaded brush – that is, about to drip – won't form a fine point.

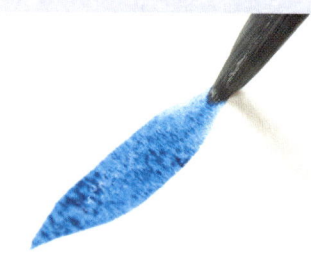

Tapering strokes Load your brush as for fine lines. Holding it upright, move the tip sideways before you touch the paper, and touch down lightly. Then, still moving, increase the pressure to broaden the stroke. Finally, gently release the pressure (still moving across the paper) and lift off.

Brush care

▶ Never put a dry brush into paint: always dampen it first.

▶ Wash your brush thoroughly after use, in cold water. Use your fingers to reshape it to a point, then leave to dry. Once dry, store your brushes in a pot with the tips upright so that the hairs will not get spoiled.

▶ Never leave your brush standing on its tip, whether in water or not, the tip will be spoiled and it is very unlikely that you will be able to straighten it.

▶ As you work, brushes will lose their point, but keep hold of older brushes – they can be useful for lifting colour washes or mixing.

 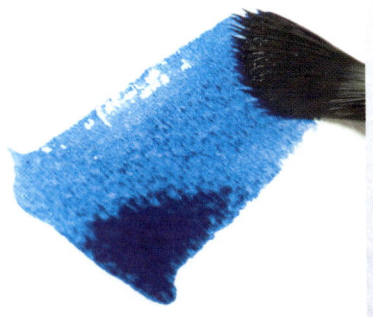 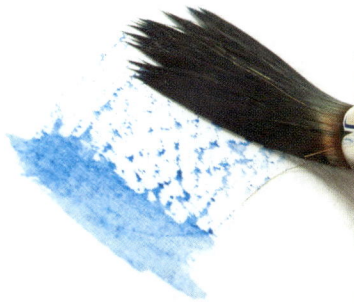

Broad lines Load your brush with plenty of paint. Holding it upright, press down gently so that the hairs curve in one direction and sweep the brush sideways across the paper in the opposite direction. Press down to make the most of the full width of the brush.

Very broad lines Load your brush, press it down onto the paper with the hairs facing away from you, and move it sideways to get a stroke that is the length of the hairs.

Dry brush Load the brush with only a little paint, and make a very broad mark. If you have difficulty with this technique, you may find it helps to hold the brush flat, as if you're about to roll it across the table, and gently skim across the paper. Your paper needs to be held flat.

Washes

Being able to create a good wash is a basic watercolour skill. A wash is simply an area of paper covered with diluted paint. For best results, do this simply and directly, using plenty of diluted paint. The result should be free of streaks and seem to 'glow' as the paper shows through the paint.

▶ A wash should only be worked into or added to while it is still damp enough to shine. If you add paint once the shine subsides, the effect is similar to when a drop of water falls from your brush onto your damp painting; you will get a blotchy watermark or 'backrun'. This occurs because the paper has already absorbed some of the water from the first wash.

▶ A common beginner's mistake is to fuss too much. If you notice a small fleck of paper unpainted, the temptation is to go back and paint it, but you may create a backrun where the new paint displaces the paint in the first wash. Leave it to dry before doing anything.

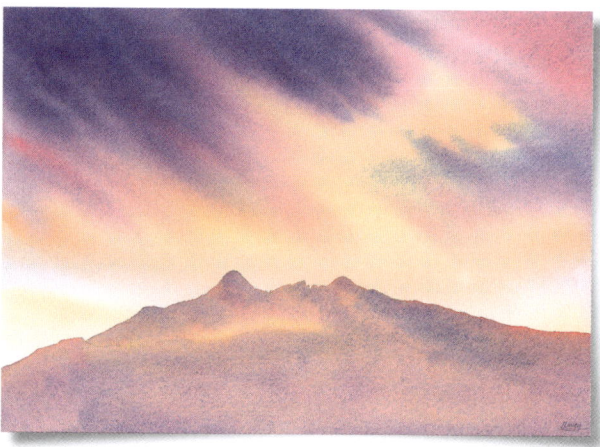

Know your materials Just three colours were used here. Colourful variegated washes (see page 14) such as this require practice, but choosing colours carefully, and knowing how they work together, can influence the outcome.

Preparing a wash

When preparing a wash, put water into the palette and add colour to it until you have the correct strength of colour. Experiment with clean water to find the amount you need to wet your sheet of paper. You can then allow the paper to dry and reuse it, knowing how much water you'll need for a wash.

When you begin to work on larger paintings you may be surprised at just how much paint you'll need for a full page. Try half a teaspoon of water as a starting point for the 15 x 10cm (6 x 4in) size of postcards in this book. Remember that the brush will take up quite a lot of paint, and allow for that.

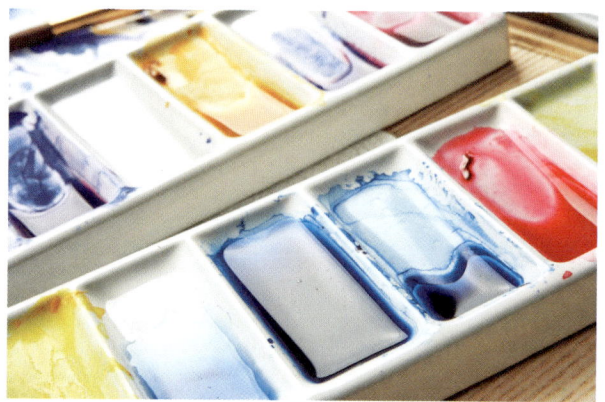

TECHNIQUE: FLAT WASH

A flat wash is a basic wash that will help you understand the importance of having plenty of paint prepared, applying it generously and leaving it to dry. Before you begin, secure your paper to a board, and set it at a slight slope in order to help the paint flow. Mix a little more paint than you think you'll need.

▶ The colour and tone of the paint should be the same throughout a flat wash. Don't wash the brush in between strokes, as this will dilute your paint.

▶ Holding the brush upright as you paint each stroke allows the paint to almost fall from the brush. If your brush starts to run out of paint before you get to the other side of the paper, quickly dip again and continue; try to use a large enough brush so that this doesn't happen.

▶ Don't worry about the little pool or bead of paint that forms at the lower edge of the wash; this prevents the paint from drying too quickly and allows the next stroke to blend smoothly into it.

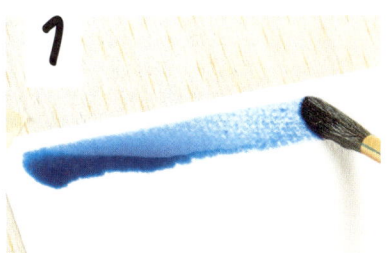

▶ Starting from the top of your paper, load your brush with paint dilute enough to form a drop at the brush tip. Draw it in a broad stroke from left to right (right to left if you're left-handed).

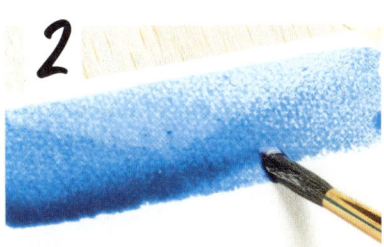

▶ Lift the brush away, then make another stroke from left to right, overlapping the previous, still wet, one. This helps to avoid streaks.

▶ When you have painted the area, dab your brush on kitchen paper to remove excess moisture and create a thirsty brush (see below). Use the tip of the brush to 'drink' any colour that is pooling at the edge. Don't press too hard or you may create a pale area in your work.

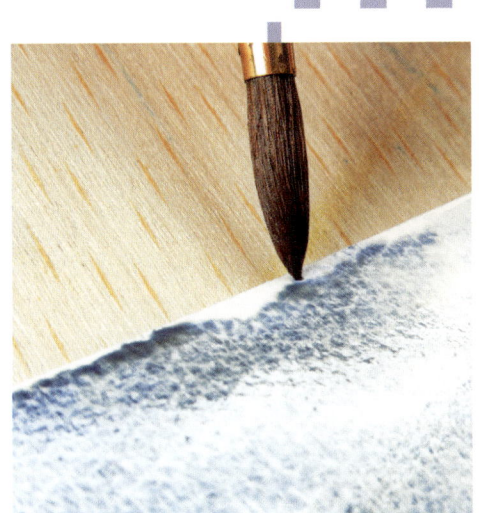

TECHNIQUE: LIFTING OUT WITH A THIRSTY BRUSH

A thirsty brush is one that is damp but has been blotted on kitchen paper to ensure that is dry enough to 'drink up' moisture – ideal for removing the bead of excess paint left at the end of a wash.

Touched to wet paint, it will draw liquid into it, which allows you to lift out wet paint in a very controlled way. Be careful to use just the tip, or you risk removing too much paint. Sable or sable/synthetic mix brushes tend to be better for this than synthetic hair brushes.

TECHNIQUE: GRADUATED WASH

The ability to produce a flat wash is a desirable skill, but the graduated wash will be more commonly used in painting mountains, as skies and landscapes vary in tone and colour.

You can also paint a graduated wash that changes in colour and tone by gradually introducing the second colour into the mix, and variegated washes where several colours are used.

▶ Prepare all the colours you need in advance for graduated washes – you don't want to run out halfway through.

▶ You can dilute the paint as you go or prepare different dilutions in your palette and use paler/weaker ones as you work down the paper. The method for applying paint to paper is the same as for a flat wash.

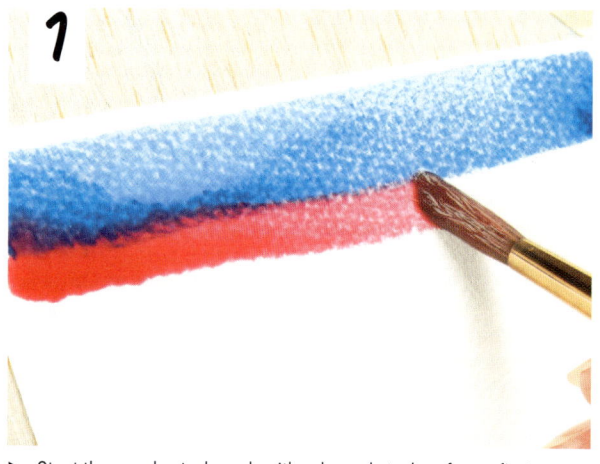

▶ Start the graduated wash with a broad stroke of your first colour. While wet, quickly rinse your brush, then load it with your second colour for subsequent strokes.

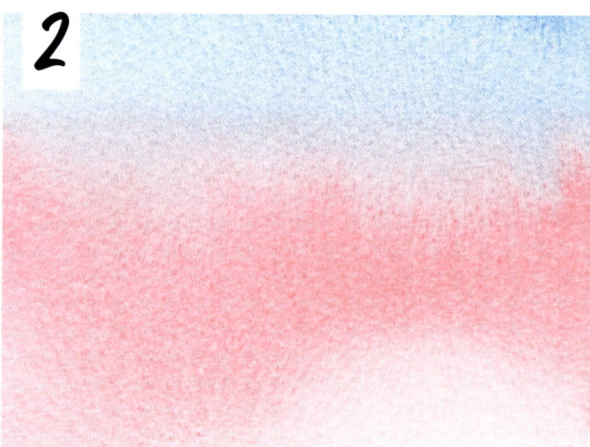

▶ Work down to the bottom of the paper, as for a flat wash. Allow to dry thoroughly.

Preparing your paper

People are often surprised when I suggest that they're struggling to achieve the result they require because they're using the wrong materials for the purpose. For example, they may be unaware that the choice of papers is key: cheap papers may cockle or disintegrate, but you can paint multiple layers on a sheet of good paper.

TECHNIQUE: GLAZING

You can create mixes of colours on the paper by overlaying a weak wash of transparent colour over another dry wash.

This is called glazing, and it can be a very effective way to create a colour that 'glows' or has a transparency that would not be achieved by other methods. The order in which your colours are laid onto the paper affects the end result: try this for yourself.

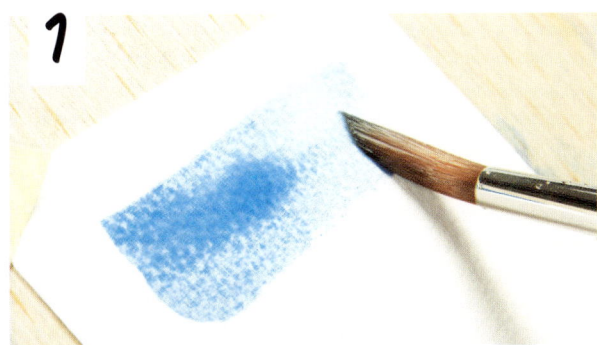

▶ Prepare and apply your first colour to the paper.

▶ Allow to dry completely, then paint your second colour over the top to create the mix. The yellow applied here appears green, as some of the blue below shows through.

Drying times

Glazing relies on the underlying paint being completely dry. When working with watercolour, drying times will vary depending on temperature and humidity. If you find the paper is drying too quickly, you can sometimes create more favourable conditions for your work by wetting the paper once, allowing the paper to 'drink', then wetting the paper again. As the paper has already absorbed some water, it will take less out of the second application.

Tone

Tone is the lightness or darkness of a colour. A sky will normally (but not always) be paler at the horizon, as will land, so your stronger tones and colours will normally be at the top and bottom of your painting.

▶ When preparing your paint, add more water to make paler tones, and add more paint to the mix for stronger tones.

▶ Building tone in layers, from light to dark, is useful for creating the illusion of distance through atmospheric perspective. It can be useful to practise this layering with one colour so that you learn to judge tones in isolation.

▶ For painting land or sea, try rotating your paper so that it is upside-down – this will ensure you can still work from dark to light. Unless sky and land are to merge together, let the sky dry before painting the land.

Simple techniques for success You can see how graduated washes were used here for the sky and sea. Once these were dry, the mountains were built up with successive flat washes glazed over the top. This gradually built up the strength of tone.

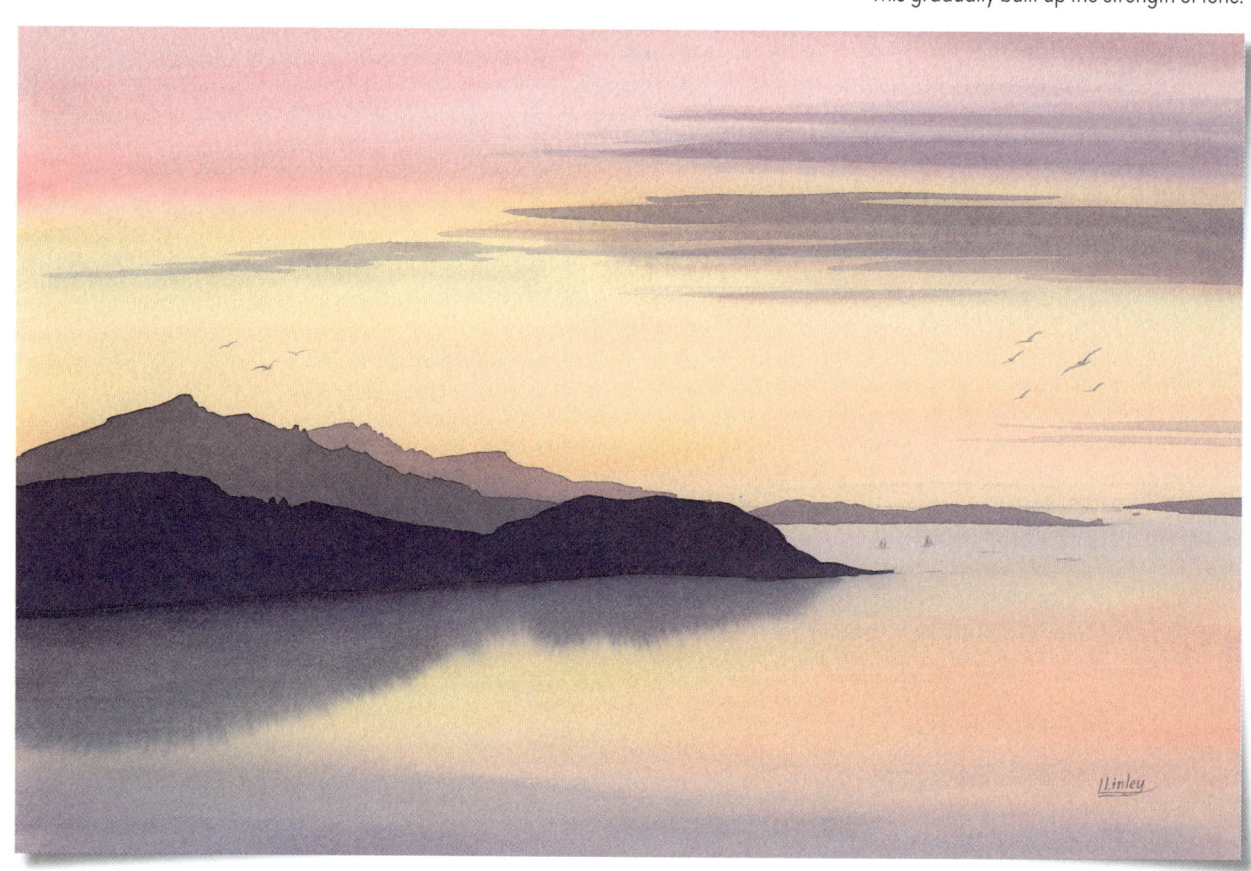

TECHNIQUE: LIFTED GLAZING

You can increase the interest in a sky by using two washes. Apply the first wash and let it dry completely, then paint a glaze over the top and lift out from that to reveal parts of the first wash.

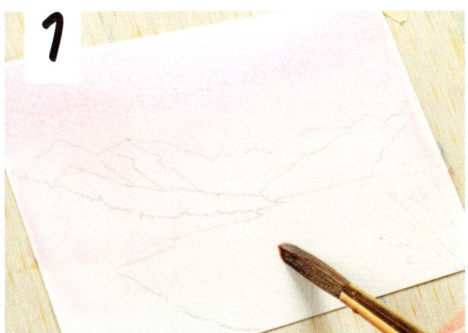

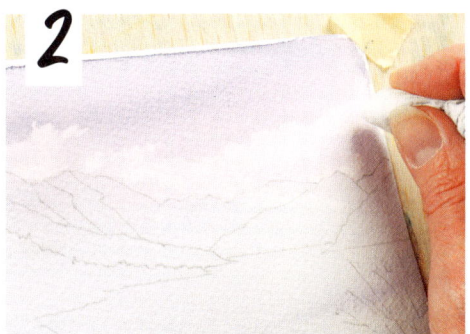

▶ Apply a pale graduated wash over the whole paper and allow to dry completely.

▶ Paint a pale graduated wash of a second colour over the whole page. While it is wet, quickly lift out clouds by dabbing areas with a piece of clean, dry kitchen paper. Make larger clouds at the top of the paper and smaller ones below.

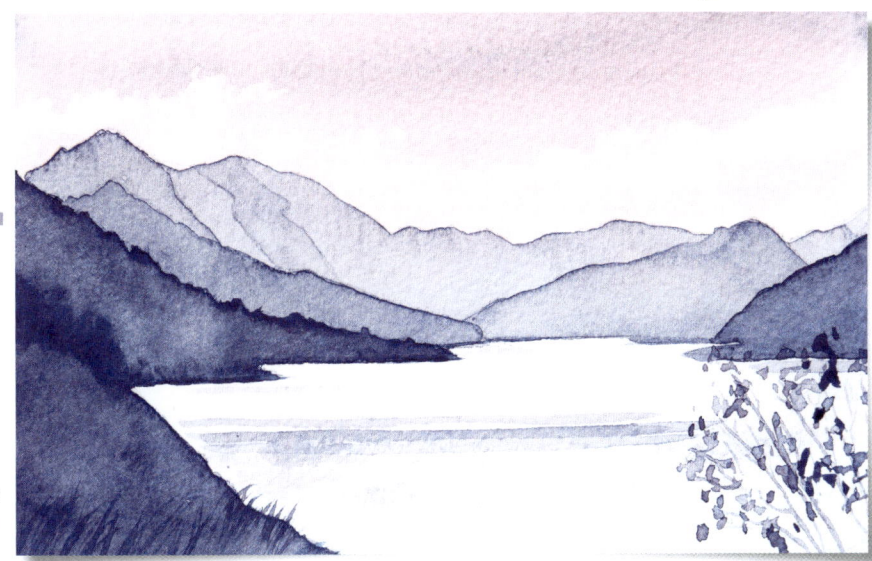

Combining techniques The effect of lifted glazing becomes clear once the stronger tones are in place. Note how the more distant mountains are painted with paler washes.

Mixing basics

You'll learn more about colour mixing if you explore what you can make from a few basics than if you buy every colour available. In fact, there is no such thing as the 'right colours' – what you choose depends on the subject you are painting and your own taste.

The primary colours of red, yellow, and blue cannot be mixed from other colours but many colours can be made from them. There are a number of ways to do this with watercolour; either in the palette, prior to applying it to the paper, or on the paper itself.

In the example to the right, areas of red, yellow and blue were painted wet into wet, creating areas of orange, green, and purple where the different colours mix on the paper.

Orange, green and purple are the secondary colours, which are the result of combining two primary colours. The precise hues you create will depend on the primary colours you use. Try painting a version using a different red, blue and yellow trio.

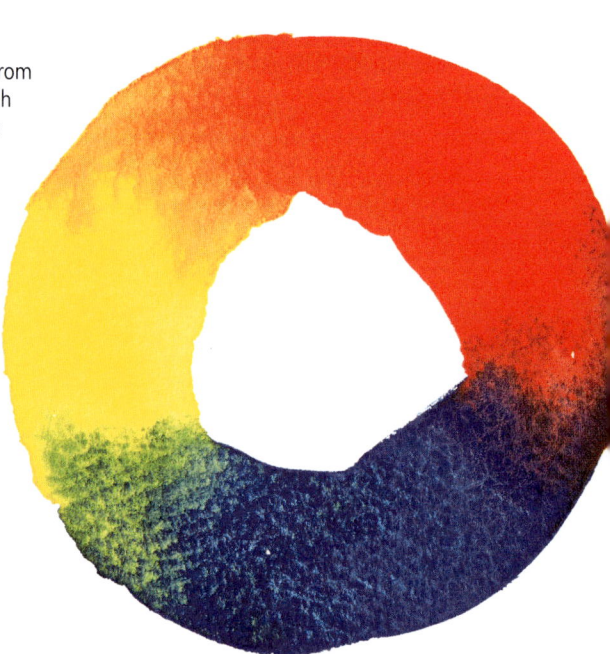

TECHNIQUE: MIXING IN THE PALETTE

Mixing in this way lets you create uniform mixes. Always add dark to light when mixing, and do so cautiously; a tiny amount of a strong colour can soon overpower a weaker or paler colour.

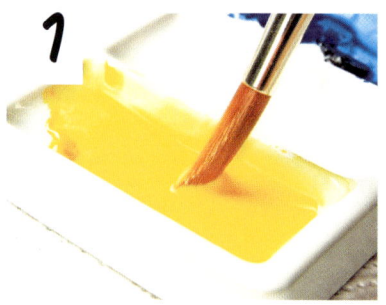

▶ Prepare a well of a light colour, such as Winsor yellow. See page 10 for preparing paint.

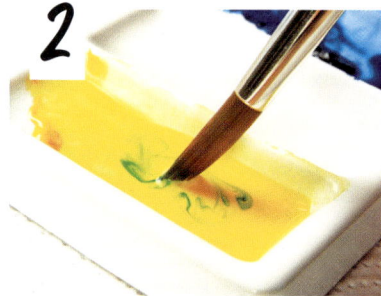

▶ Clean the brush and pick up a small amount of a darker colour – Prussian blue, here – into the well.

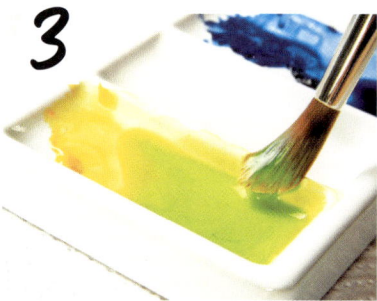

▶ Mix well until you get a consistent colour, then you can start to paint.

Choosing your colours

I use a dozen colours (see right) and know how they behave on my paper. Knowing which mixes give bright colours and which give subdued colours will save a lot of disappointment.

I often combine French ultramarine with burnt umber to produce an interesting natural grey mix; these colours work well for me for rocks, clouds or water. Mixing two colours rather than buying a ready-mixed uniform grey means that I'm able to have a variety of shades of blue/brown in the warm and cool greys that form, rather than simply different tones of the same colour.

▶ My core palette includes a warm and cool version of each primary colour, giving a wider range of colours from mixing than if just one red, yellow and blue were used. These are Winsor lemon, Winsor yellow, permanent rose, scarlet lake, French ultramarine and Winsor blue (green shade).

▶ In addition to the colours in my core palette, I use raw sienna, burnt umber, burnt sienna, quinacridone gold, Prussian blue and cobalt blue.

Getting familiar with your colours

Creating a simple chart like mine below will help you to practise mixing. Keep the brush well rinsed between mixes, and the paint on your palette clean. The colours used here are simply examples; you can substitute whatever colours you like.

You do not need to fill in all the boxes, as they simply repeat. Note the diagonal line of unmixed colours where their names appear as both the row and column headers.

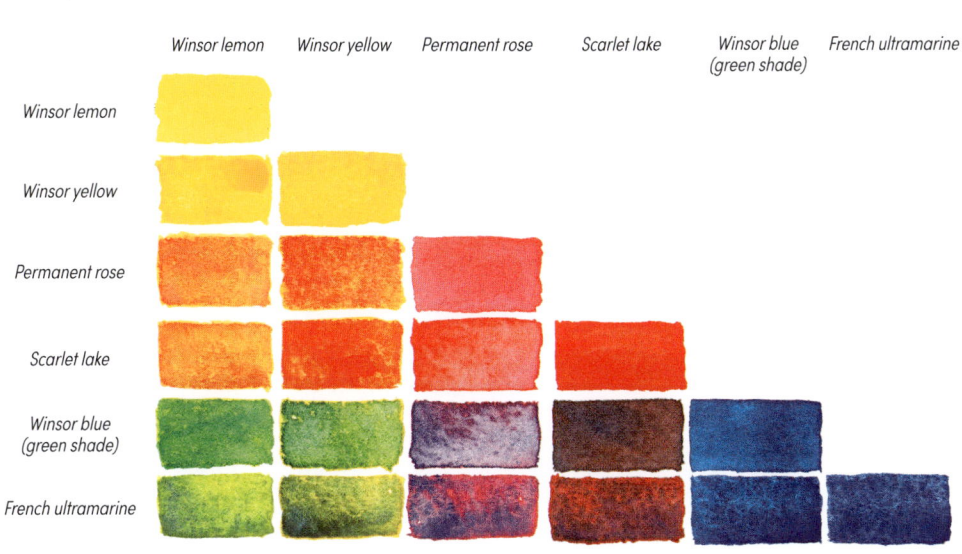

TECHNIQUE: WET INTO WET

As well as mixing colours on the palette, you can mix them on the paper. This can be done wet on dry through glazing (see page 15), or you can allow one colour to blend into another on the paper while it is still wet.

Here, fresh wet paint was added below the still-wet mountains. The areas were drawn together with the brush and allowed to bleed together, giving a soft, hazy result rather than a hard edge.

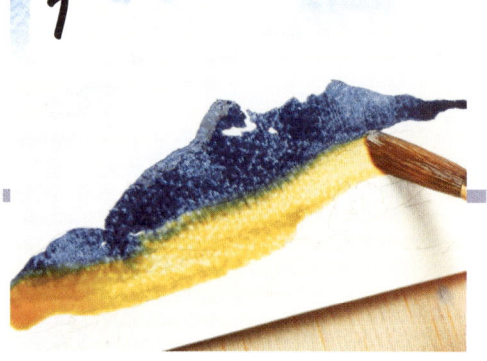

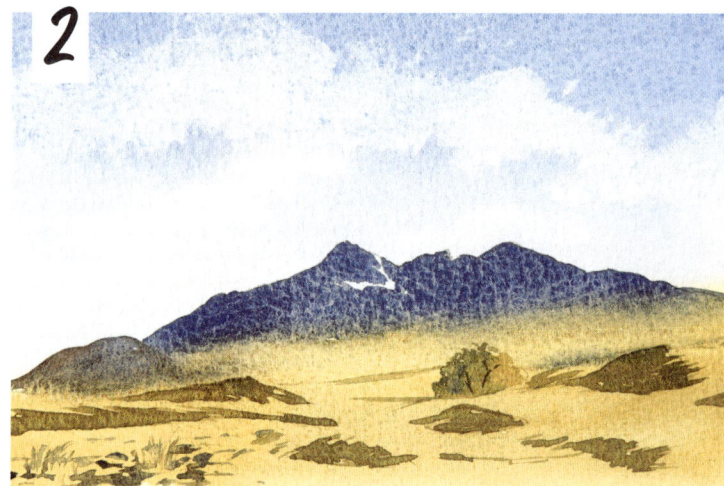

Paint strength

Remember, watercolour dries to a paler tone than it appears when wet. This is particularly important to remember when working wet into wet, as the already-wet surface increases the dilution of the paint, making the result paler than you might expect. Prepare your paints accordingly.

TECHNIQUE: DROPPING IN

Dropping in involves putting the tip of a loaded brush into a particular wet area of the paper and allowing the colour to spread onto the paper naturally. If left alone, the paint diffuses into the wet surface to give a wonderful soft result.

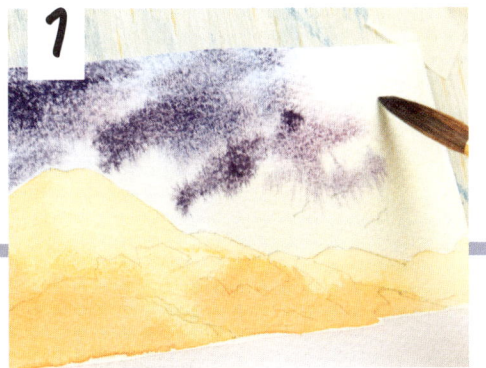

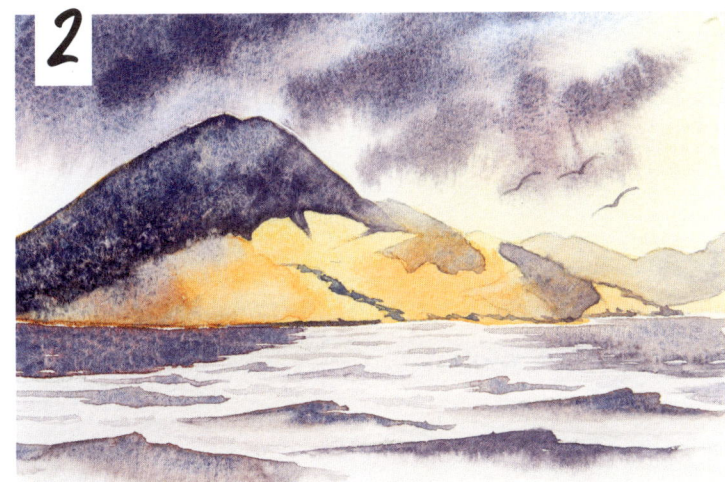

Using two brushes

Using more than one brush saves time when switching between colours, or between applying washes and more detailed work, like drawing out fine lines from a wash. If you use the same brush for both tasks, you need to remove surplus paint from the brush each time you switch.

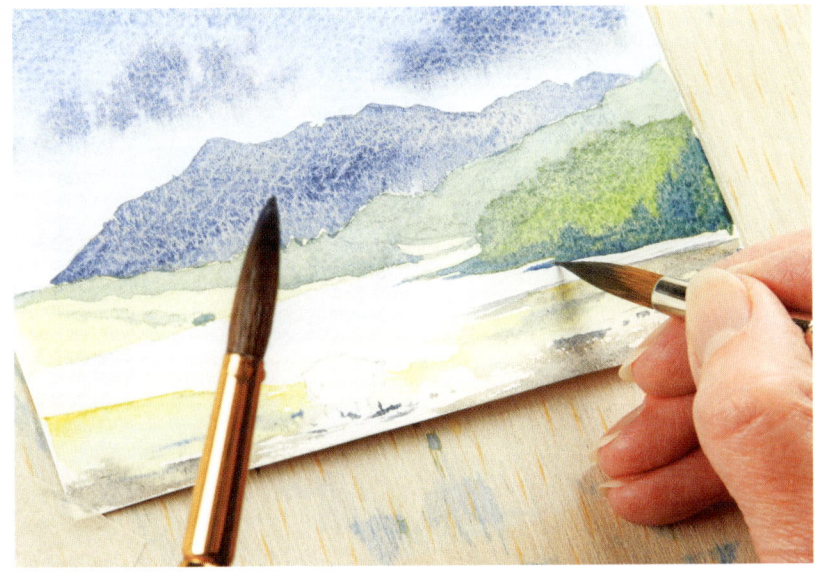

Reserving highlights

I use Saunders Waterford rag paper ('rag' means it is made from cotton, rather than wood fibre) for my paintings. The High White version (whiter than Traditional White) gives me the extra brightness I need because I don't use white paint: the white of the paper itself serves as a bright area.

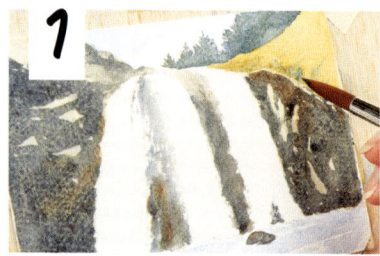

▶ When painting, be careful to leave your highlights – don't overpaint the gaps.

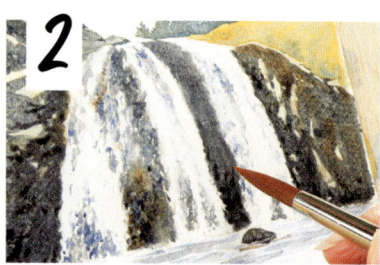

▶ Don't worry if you do go slightly over the areas you want to be light: if necessary, you can lift out additional highlights with a thirsty brush.

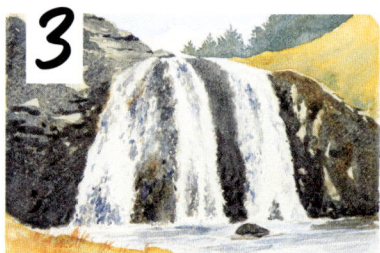

▶ The highlights in this finished picture are simply the clean white paper, which has remained untouched for the whole process.

TECHNIQUE: SPLITTING THE BRUSH

For grasses, instead of using a fan-shaped brush, you can load a little paint on your round brush. Gently press the hairs between your fingers to form a rough fan shape, as shown below left.

Put brush to paper, and flick the brush in the direction of growth for the grass. Move the hairs around to avoid a stencil/repeat pattern effect.

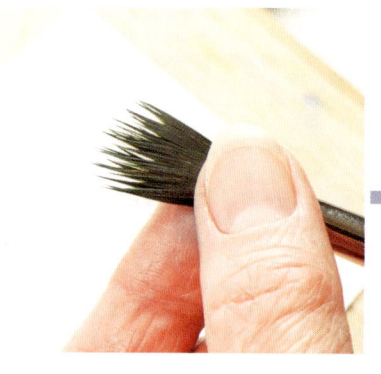

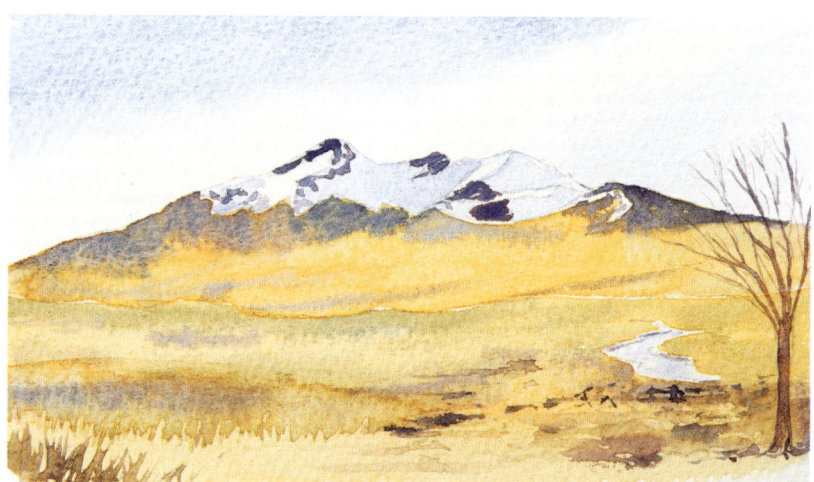

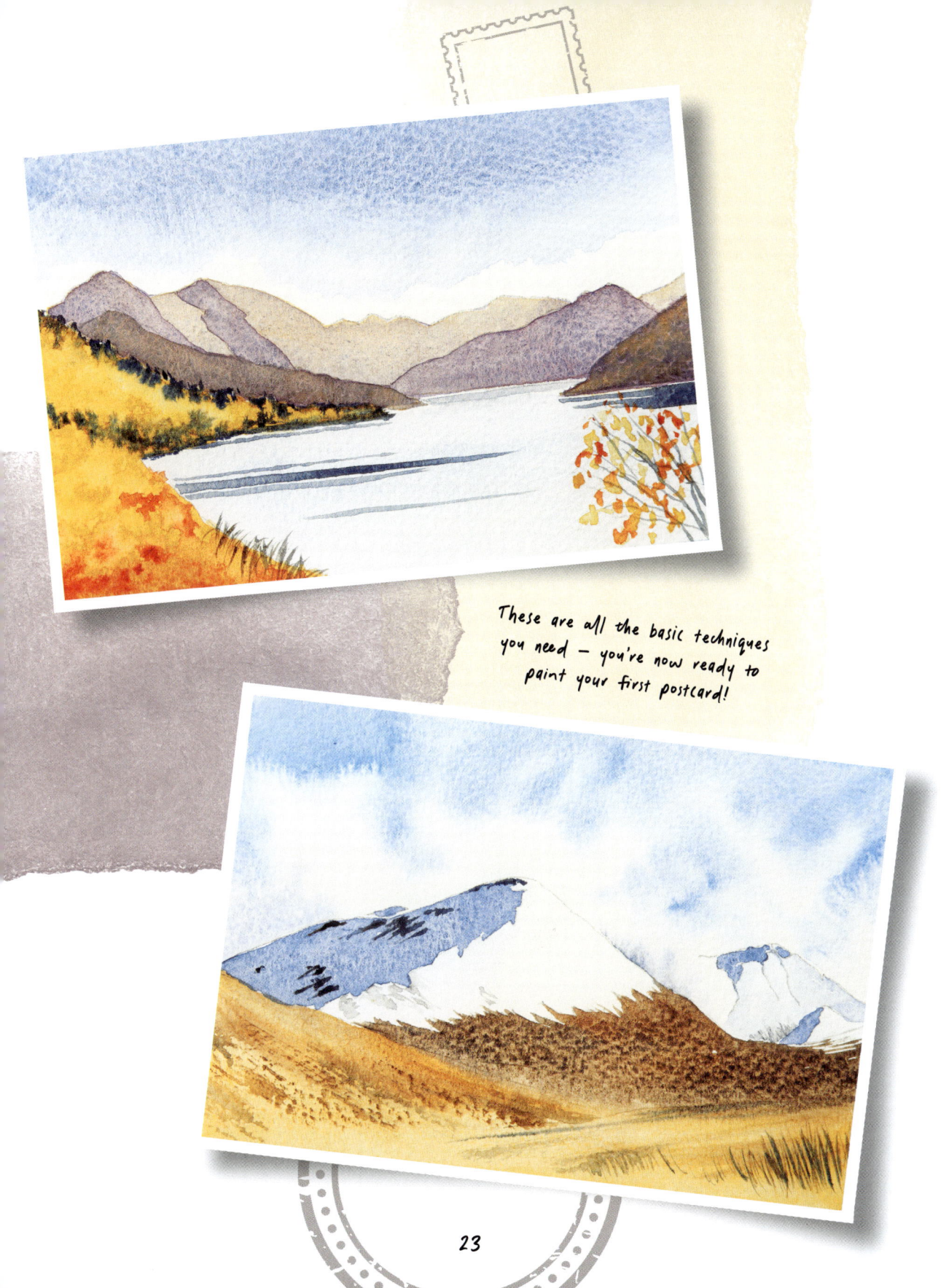

These are all the basic techniques
you need — you're now ready to
paint your first postcard!

Summer Sky

A clear blue sky, with clouds lifted out from the wet wash, provides a simple but effective first step to painting skies.

When mixing French ultramarine and burnt umber, add the burnt umber a little at a time: it's a strong colour that can quickly overpower the blue.

YOU WILL NEED

Paint colours: French ultramarine, raw sienna, burnt umber

Brush: size 10 round

Other: outline drawing on page 85 (top), kitchen paper

TECHNIQUE: GRANULATION

This painting uses French ultramarine, a colour that gives a beautiful mottled effect called granulation. This is a characteristic of the paint, and caused by the particles of paint sinking into the textured surface of the paper.

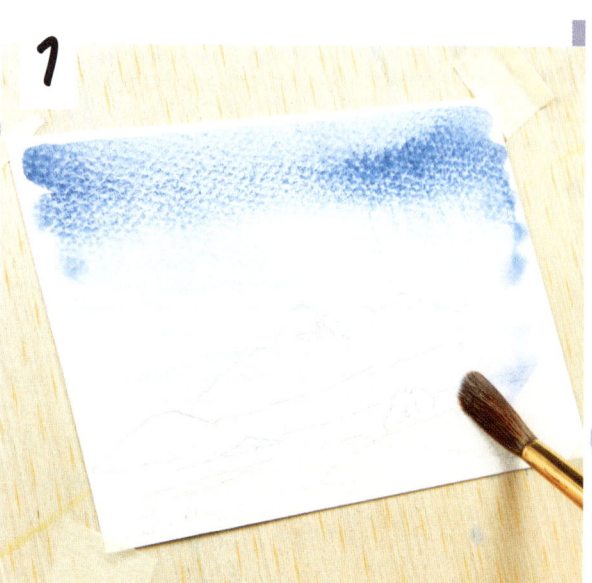

1

▶ Have a piece of kitchen paper handy, crumpled into a ball. Secure your paper to the board, then paint the paper all over with a graduated wash of French ultramarine, introducing pure water instead of a second colour. This will result in the sky becoming gradually paler as it drops below the horizon.

Watching paint dry

There are times when we really need to watch paint dry in order to avoid backruns, or to judge the degree of dampness for the effect we require. If you wish to work wet into wet, you need to learn how to judge this crucial stage by observation – watching paint dry – and experimenting with different colours and dilutions. A stronger mix will spread less than a very weak one of the same colour, while some colours spread more readily than others. Practise to see how they soften or spread into a wash.

TECHNIQUE: LIFTING OUT

Lifting out is the controlled removal of wet paint using kitchen paper, as shown here. You can also lift out dry paint using a combination of brush and kitchen paper (see page 38). The degree of success – that is, how much paint is removed – will depend on the colour and paper used.

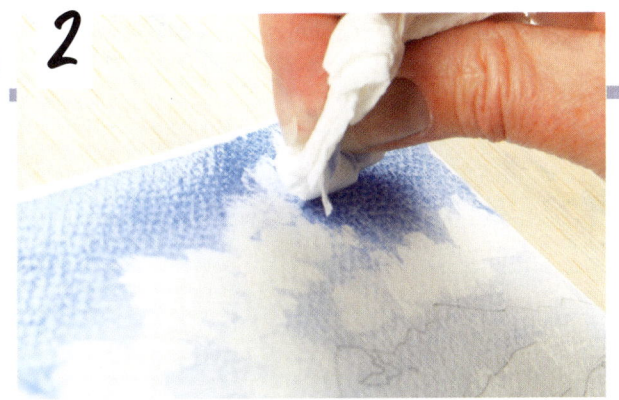

▶ While it is still damp, lift out cloud shapes with the kitchen paper, making larger clouds at the top and smaller ones lower down. Work quickly and turn the kitchen paper frequently so that you don't put the paint back onto the painting. Allow to dry.

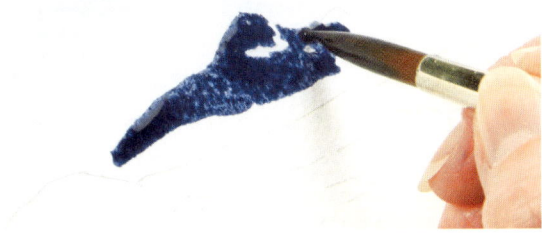

▶ Paint the hills with a mix of French ultramarine and burnt umber, omitting the white area.

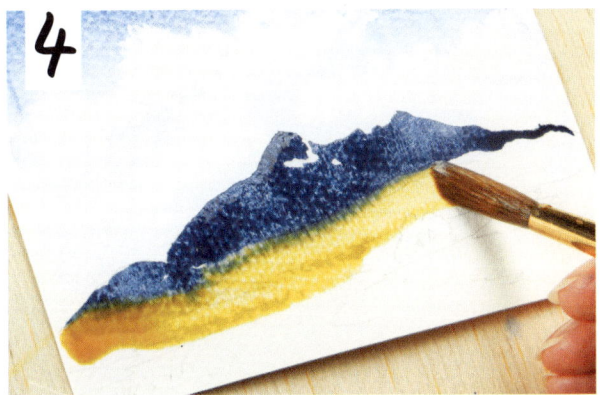

▶ While the hills are still wet, paint the moorland below with pale raw sienna, allowing the two colours to blend on the paper.

5

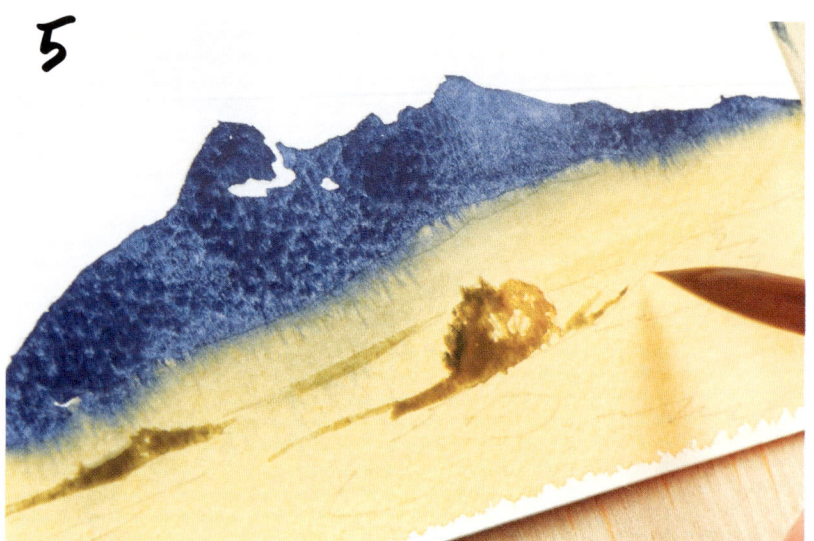

▶ Using a raw sienna and French ultramarine mix, paint the shadow sides of the mounds. For the shrub, use raw sienna and then a little French ultramarine, placing the colour in tiny dots – see stippling, above right – and allow them to touch so that the colours can merge.

TECHNIQUE: STIPPLING

Stippling is simply making lots of tiny dots of colour near to one another. It is useful for creating variation of colour in foliage, or to suggest small rocks and pebbles.

6

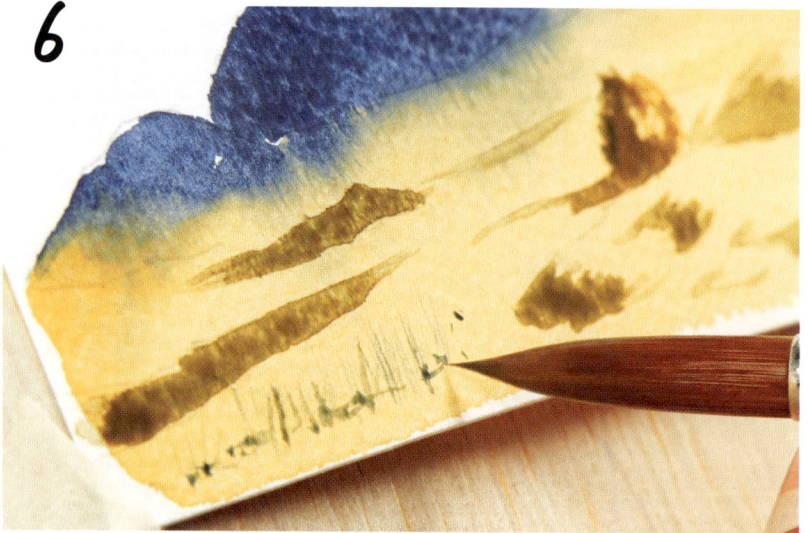

▶ Add a few grass/stone details using a French ultramarine and burnt umber mix. Simply paint numerous fine lines, starting at the base of the grasses and flicking the brush towards the top – that is, in the direction of growth. For a solid 'base', finish with a horizontal line.

TECHNIQUE: FINE GRASSES

Patches of grass and similar plants add interest, scale and variation to a landscape. The key is to make lots of fine 'flicked' lines. Avoid adding too many – less is more – and add them only in the foreground.

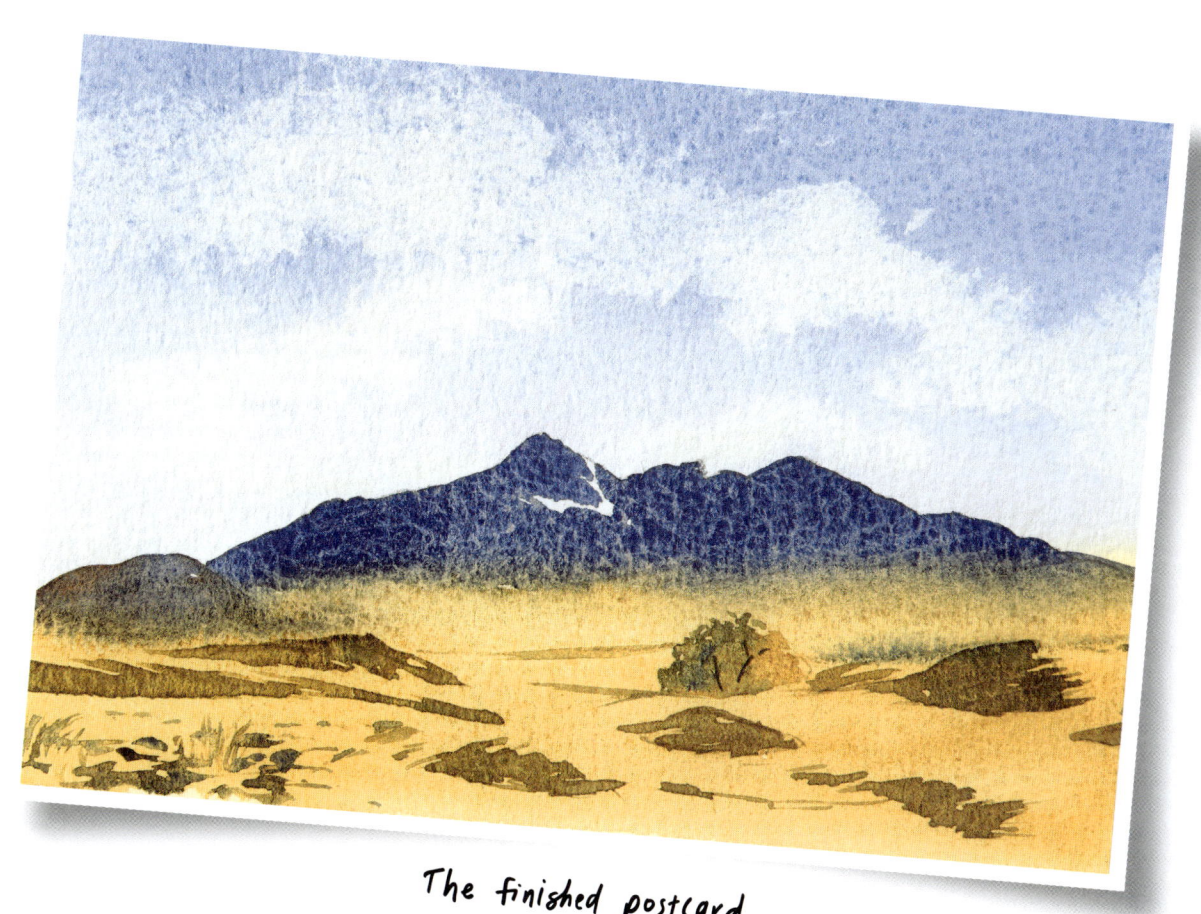

The finished postcard

Colourful Clouds

Capturing the effect of sunlight and shadows on billowing clouds may seem daunting, but it can be quite simple if you plan your work. The clouds are painted 'negatively', that is, created by the blue painting around them; and the colours within them placed carefully to avoid the likelihood of unfortunate colour blends. Here, placing the pink clouds next to the yellow keeps the blue separate from the yellow, reducing the chance of green clouds occurring.

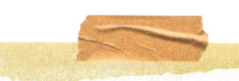

YOU WILL NEED

Paint colours: French ultramarine, raw sienna, permanent rose

Brush: size 10 round

Other: outline drawing on page 85 (bottom), putty eraser

Negative and positive painting

Positive painting is simply picking out features directly – painting a cloud itself, for example – while negative painting is suggesting the shape of an object by painting the area around it. Here, we suggest the cloud by painting the sky behind it – an example of negative painting.

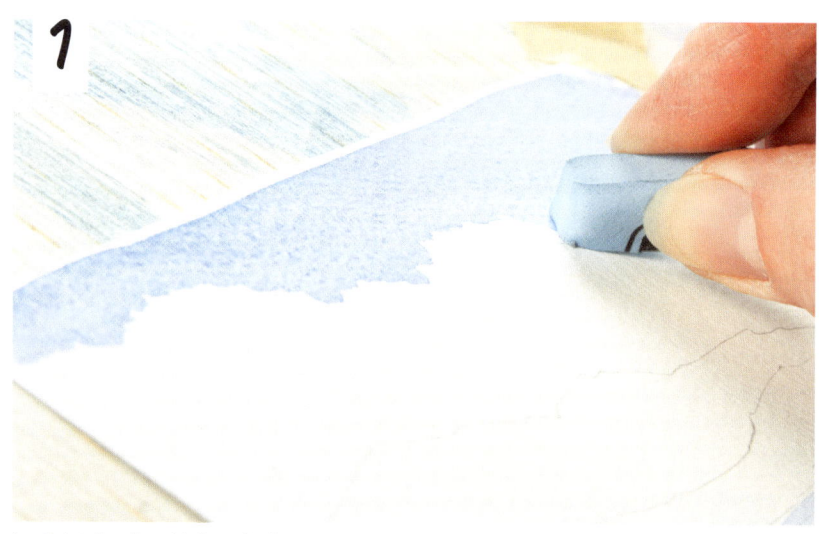

1

▶ Paint the sky with French ultramarine, quickly creating a ragged edge for the clouds before the paint dries. Soften the cloud edge on the right with a clean damp brush. Aim to paint up to, but not over, the pencil lines. Once dry, use a soft eraser to remove the pencil line. It isn't always necessary or desirable to remove pencil, but there are some occasions when it is best removed, particularly when the surrounding areas are very light in tone.

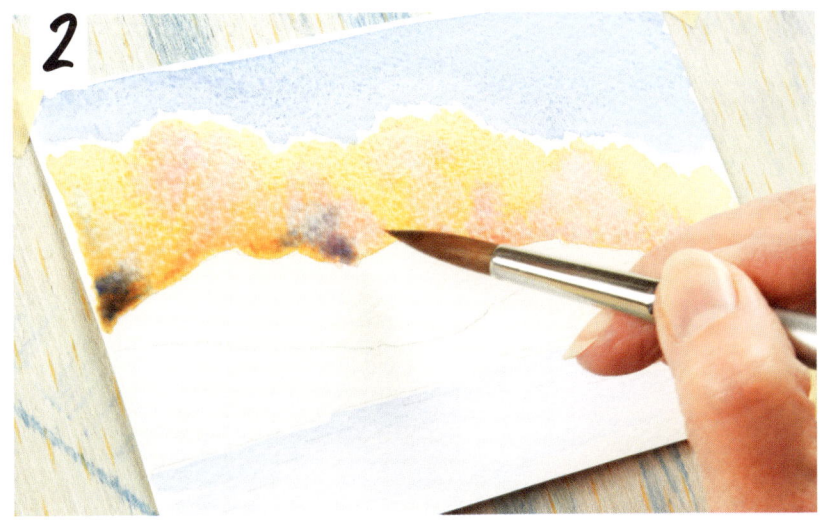

▶ Paint the sea with very pale French ultramarine, leaving a few thin horizontal lines of clean, dry paper. Paint the cloud with pale raw sienna, leaving a ragged white line at the top edge, then drop in permanent rose, and add French ultramarine to the pink area for the darker areas of the cloud.

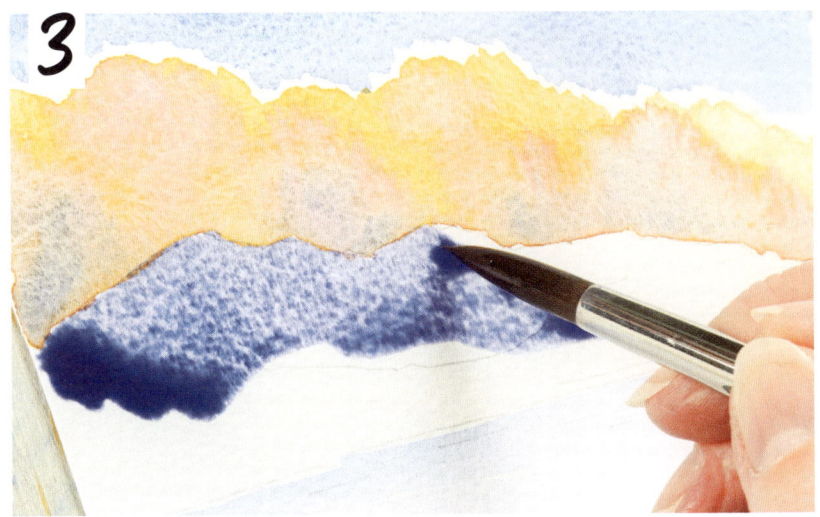

▶ With a mix of French ultramarine and a little permanent rose, paint in the land mass.

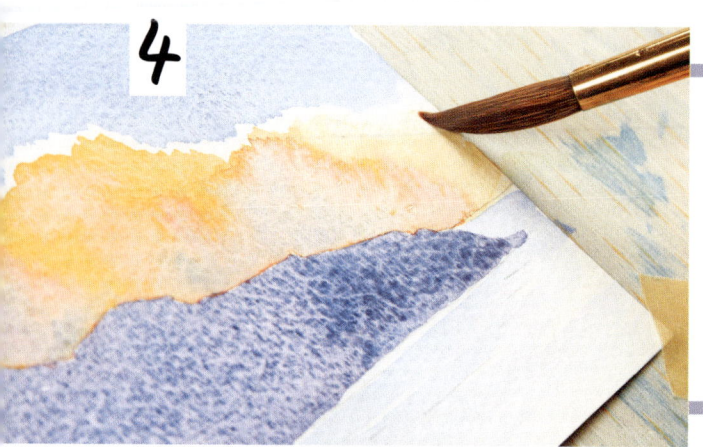

4

TECHNIQUE: SOFTENING

To soften an edge, use a clean, damp brush to draw the colour away from the edge of the wash. The amount of water is critical: if your brush is damp, you will gently encourage the paint to move; but if your brush is very wet and you push it into the wash, you're likely to create a backrun as the pigment is lifted and pushed out of the way.

▶ Soften the top right-hand edge of the cloud using a clean, damp brush.

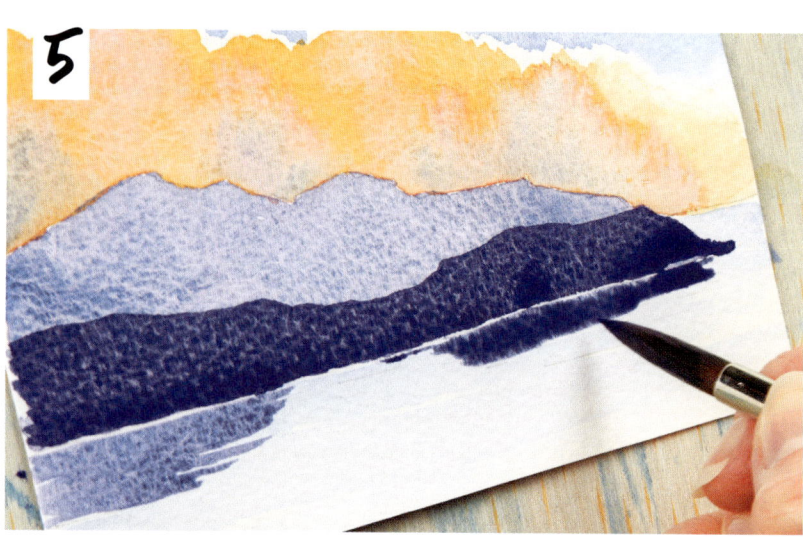

5

▶ Glaze the nearer land mass with a stronger mix. Add a few horizontal lines to suggest reflections in the sea, leaving a thin white line at the shore.

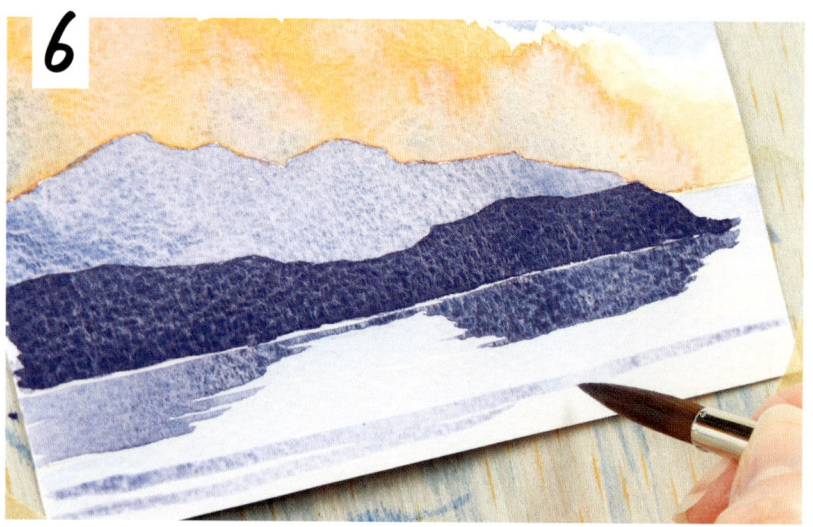

6

▶ Add a few lines of French ultramarine to the lower part of the sea to reflect the blue area of the sky. Add a touch of pale permanent rose here and there, but leave some areas unpainted on the sea to reveal the pale wash underneath.

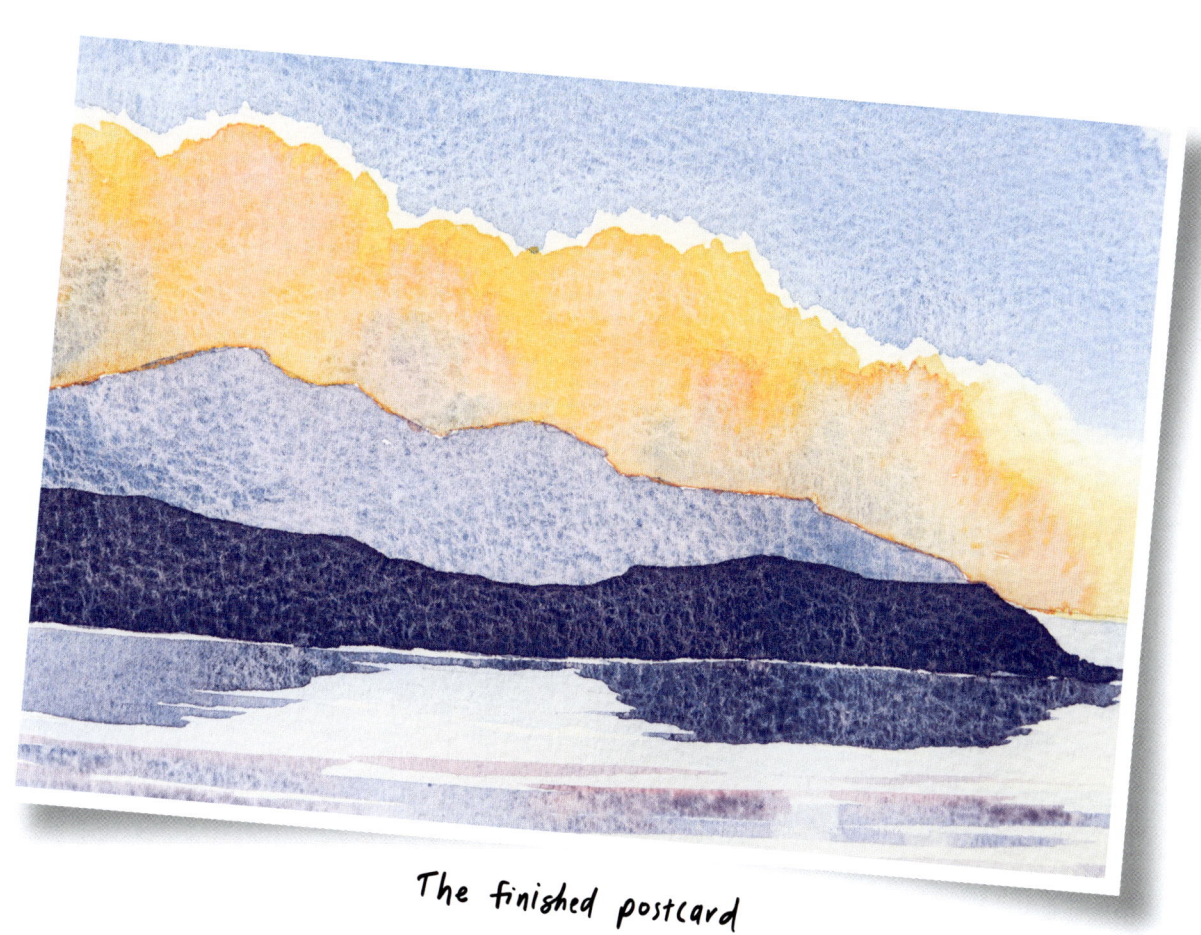

The finished postcard

Colour and Distance

This scene explores colour temperature. Advancing (warmer colours) and receding (cooler) colours are used here to create a feeling of distance.

Familiarity with the scene means you can push yourself to work more swiftly, so we introduce the technique of leaving gaps between areas to speed up your pace. Here the cloud band gives a natural gap.

YOU WILL NEED

Paint colours: raw sienna, burnt sienna, permanent rose, burnt umber, French ultramarine

Brush: size 10 round

Other: outline drawing on page 86

TECHNIQUE: LEAVING GAPS FOR SPEED

Leaving thin slivers of unpainted paper between adjacent washes means that one cannot run into another. This eliminates the need for the first wash to dry before moving on to the next, thus increasing speed.

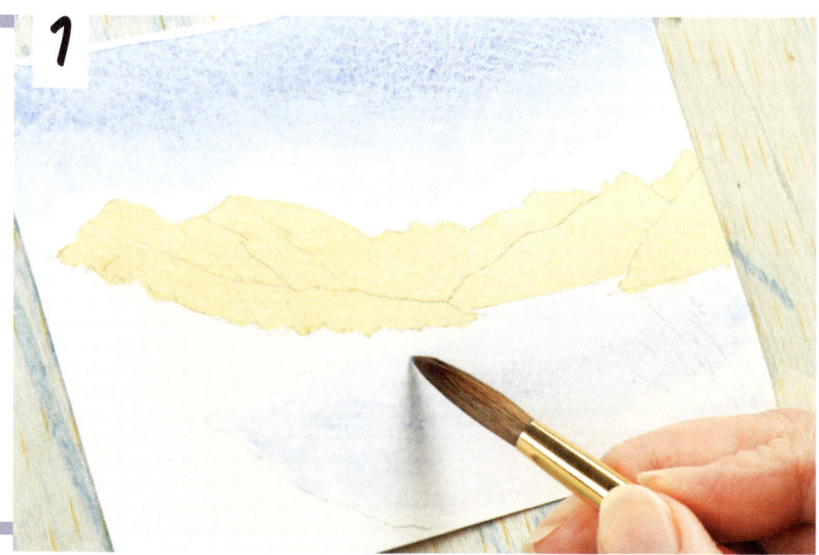

1

▶ Using French ultramarine and a graduated wash, paint the sky above the cloud band; then with raw sienna, paint the mountains. (It should be safe to do this if you left a band of cloud above all the peaks.) With pale French ultramarine, paint the sea, leaving a thin line unpainted at the shoreline.

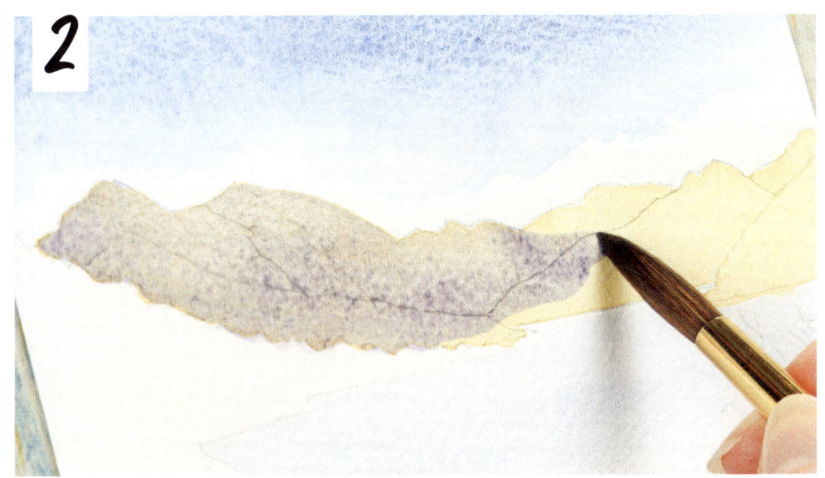

► Paint the mountains again, this time using a pale mix of French ultramarine and permanent rose.

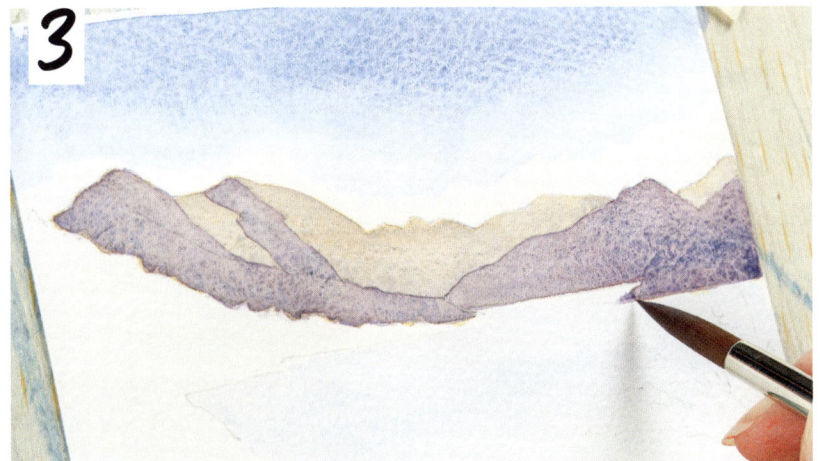

► Once more, using the same colours, paint the mountains as shown.

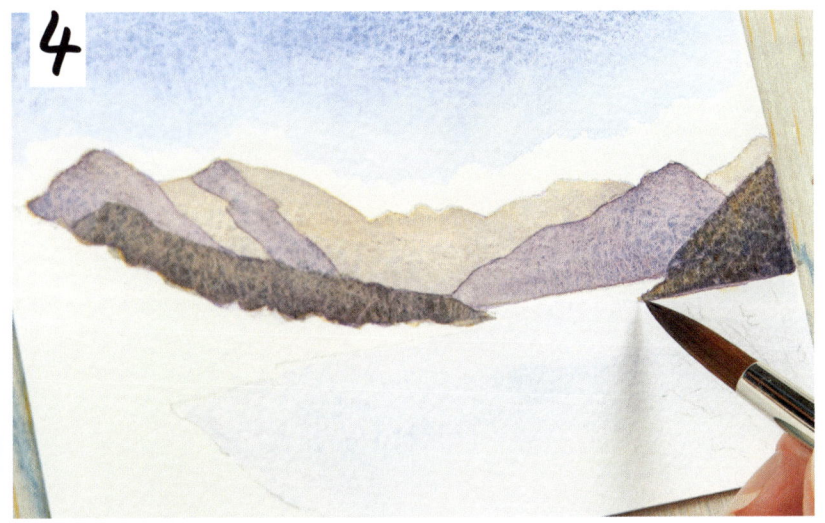

► Once dry, paint the nearer mountains with a mix of raw sienna, permanent rose and French ultramarine.

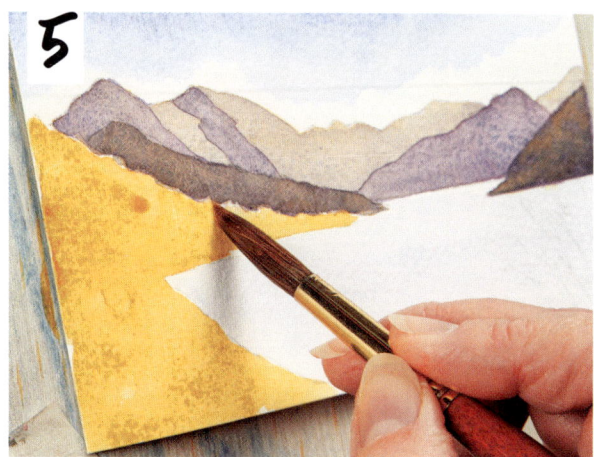

▶ Beginning with raw sienna, paint the trees and bank on the left.

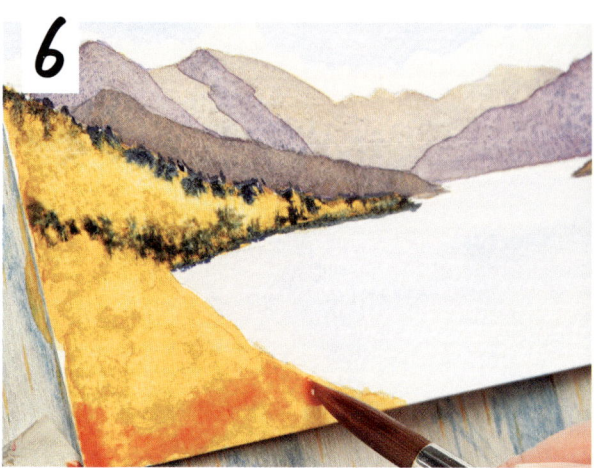

▶ While the wash is damp, add burnt sienna and French ultramarine here and there, allowing the colours to blend. Add a mix of French ultramarine and burnt umber as the paint dries so that the colour will spread less.

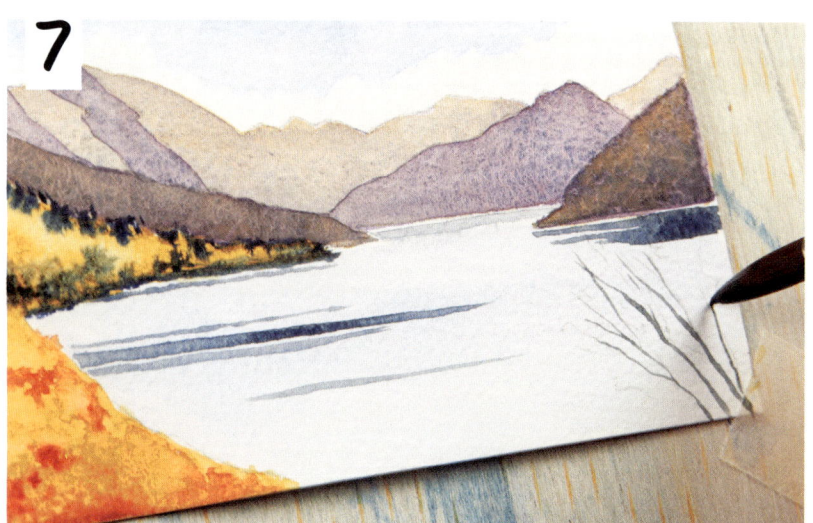

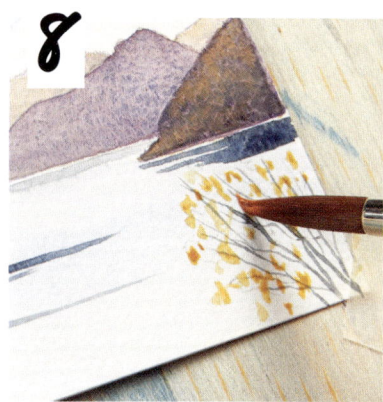

▶ Create the leaves with dots and dabs of raw sienna and burnt sienna, allowing the colours to bleed into one another.

▶ Add some horizontal lines to the sea with a mix of French ultramarine and burnt umber, and paint the branches of the tree in the foreground with the same mix. Use just a little paint on the brush so that you get a good point, and paint the twigs in the direction of growth.

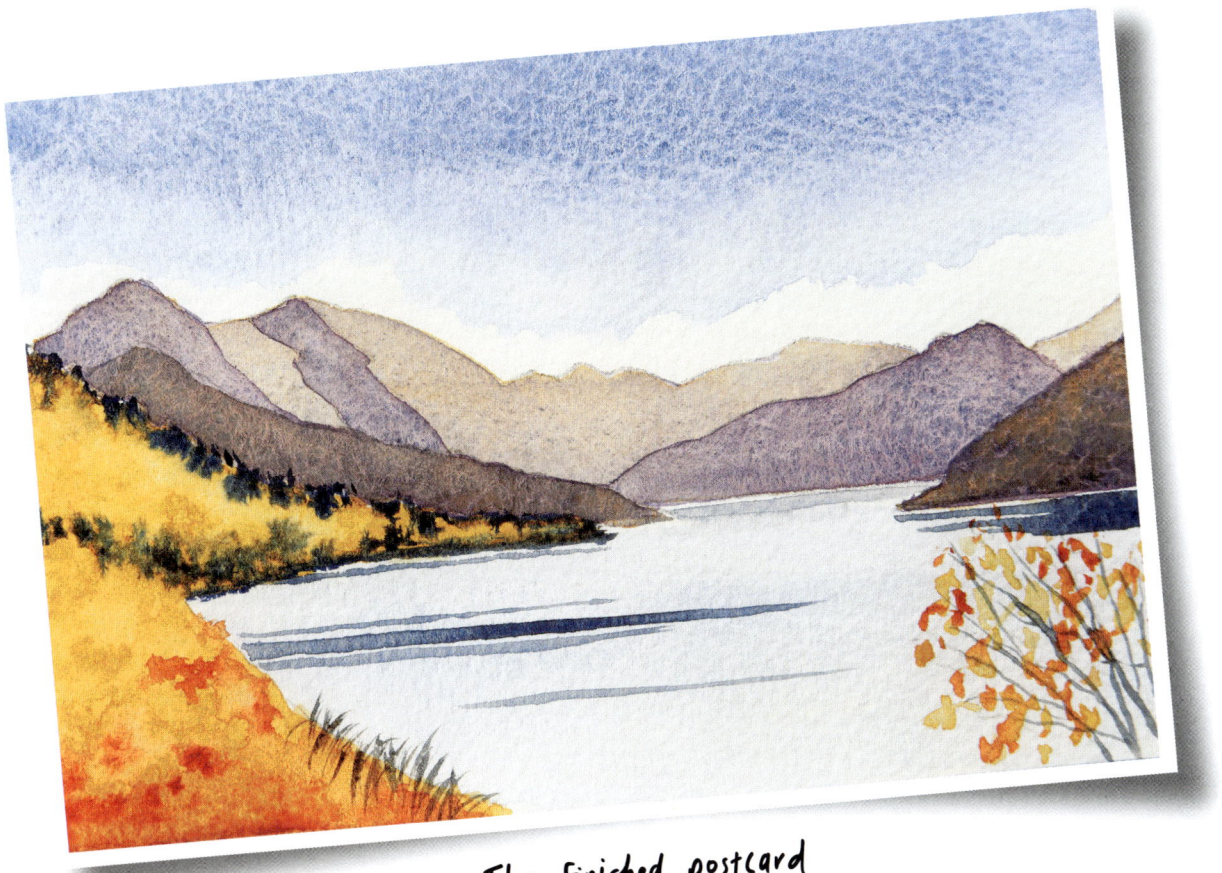

The finished postcard

Let light through

Add more paint to the leaves to strengthen the colours, if you wish, but try to leave the sea colour showing through some of the leaves.

Waterfall

Creating texture on rock need not be complicated. By using the natural granulation that occurs with this mix, putting washes on and leaving the colours to 'do their magic', the textures are created for us. Tones are built with more layers of the same mix. The colours will separate a little in your palette; it can be pleasing to allow this (by not stirring up the colours too often), rather than have flat colour throughout.

YOU WILL NEED

Paint colours: burnt umber, French ultramarine

Brush: size 10 round

Other: outline drawing on page 87

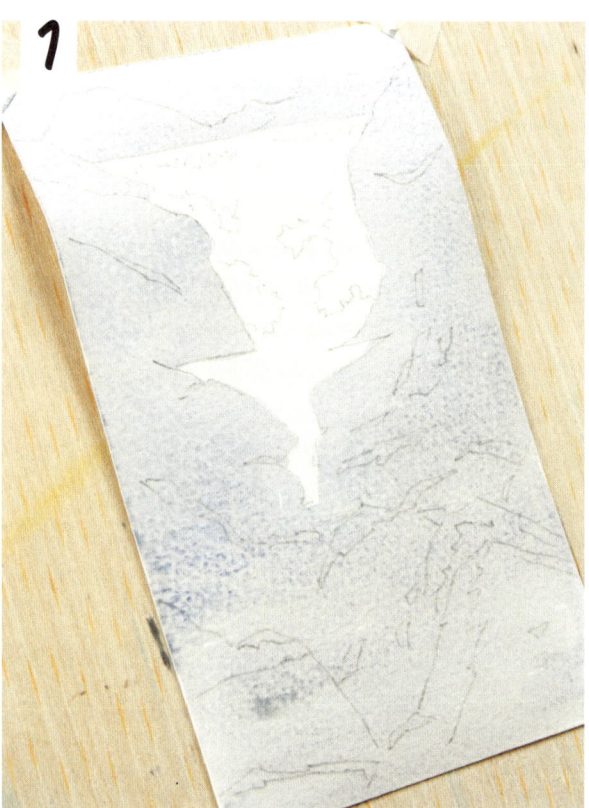

▶ Make a pale mix of the colours and paint everything except the waterfall.

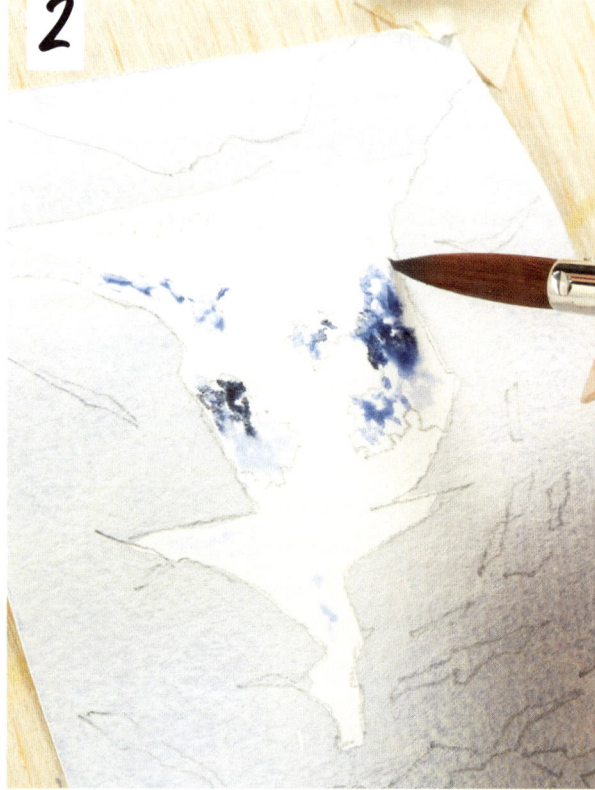

▶ Stipple a few dots of pale French ultramarine on the waterfall and allow some of these to join up. Add a few dots of stronger French ultramarine and burnt umber.

3

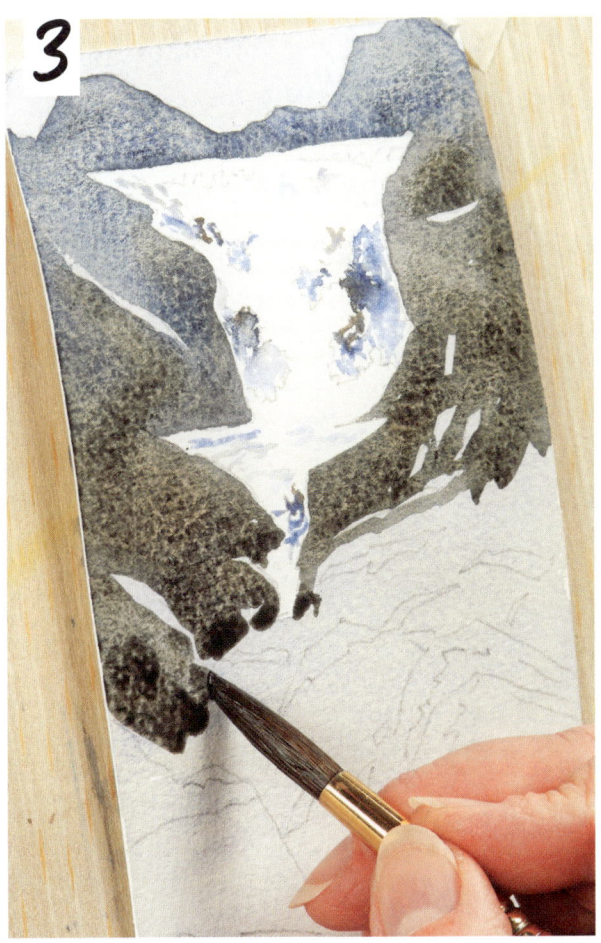

▶ Use a stronger tone of the mix to paint the rocks. Starting from the top with a blue-biased mix, work down while gradually changing to a brown-biased mix. Leave the lightest areas of the rocks unpainted: keep the paint wet so that one area flows into another. This also allows the paint to granulate.

4

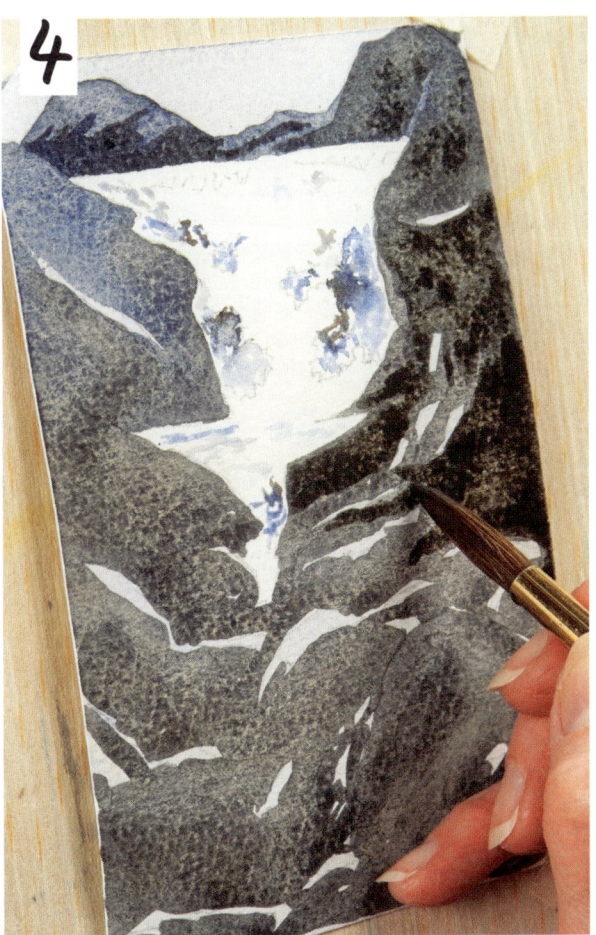

▶ Once the rocks are dry, use a darker mix to overpaint the darker areas of all the rocks, again keeping the paint very fluid on the page. Drop in stronger darks here and there to further vary the tone.

Re-tracing

If your lines have been lost under the first wash, you can allow the painting to dry and re-trace them. Alternatively, as there's no 'correct' shape for a rock, you could just do your best without the lines.

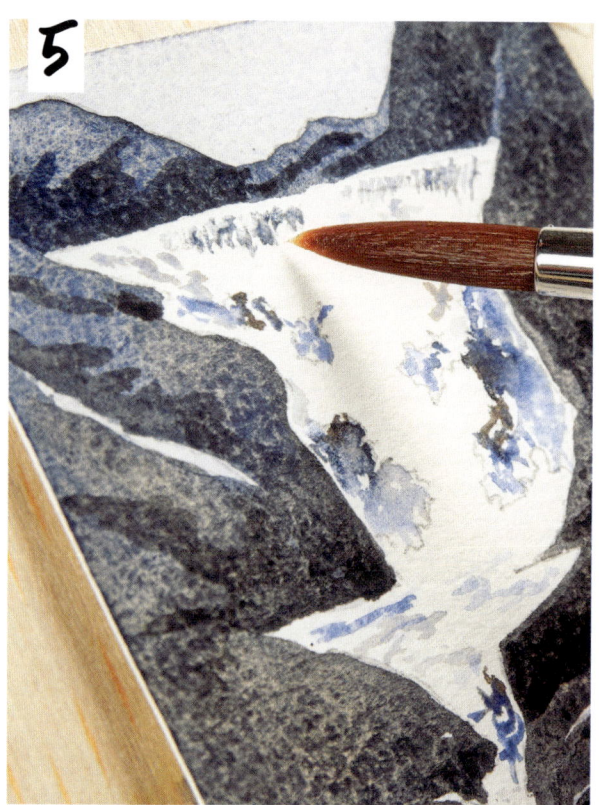

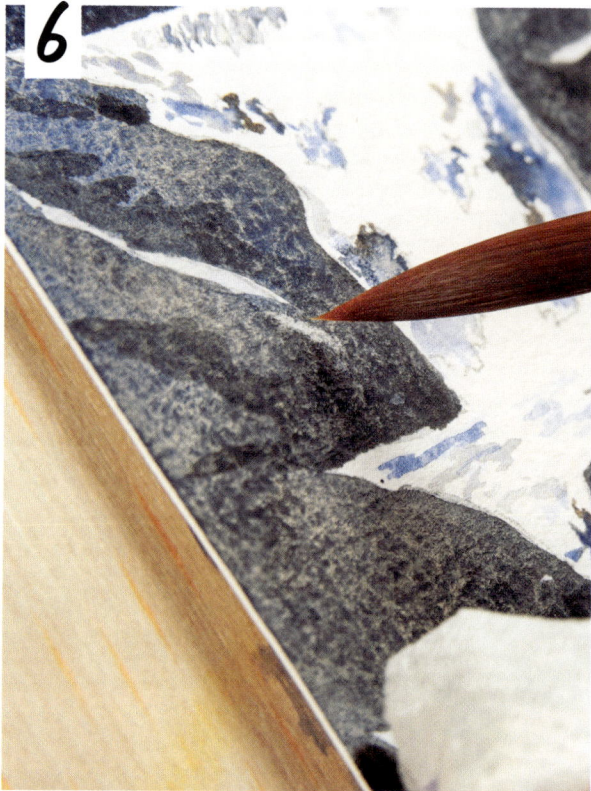

▶ Add the darker details to the top of the waterfall with short marks that follow the curve of the waterfall. Use the same mix as for the rocks, but slightly diluted. This helps to give the illusion that parts of the rocks are visible through bright, clear, foaming water.

▶ Lift out a few highlights from the dry paint of the rocks using a damp brush to loosen the paint and kitchen paper to blot. Avoid creating soft, fuzzy edges – use the point of your brush to create sharp, angular highlights.

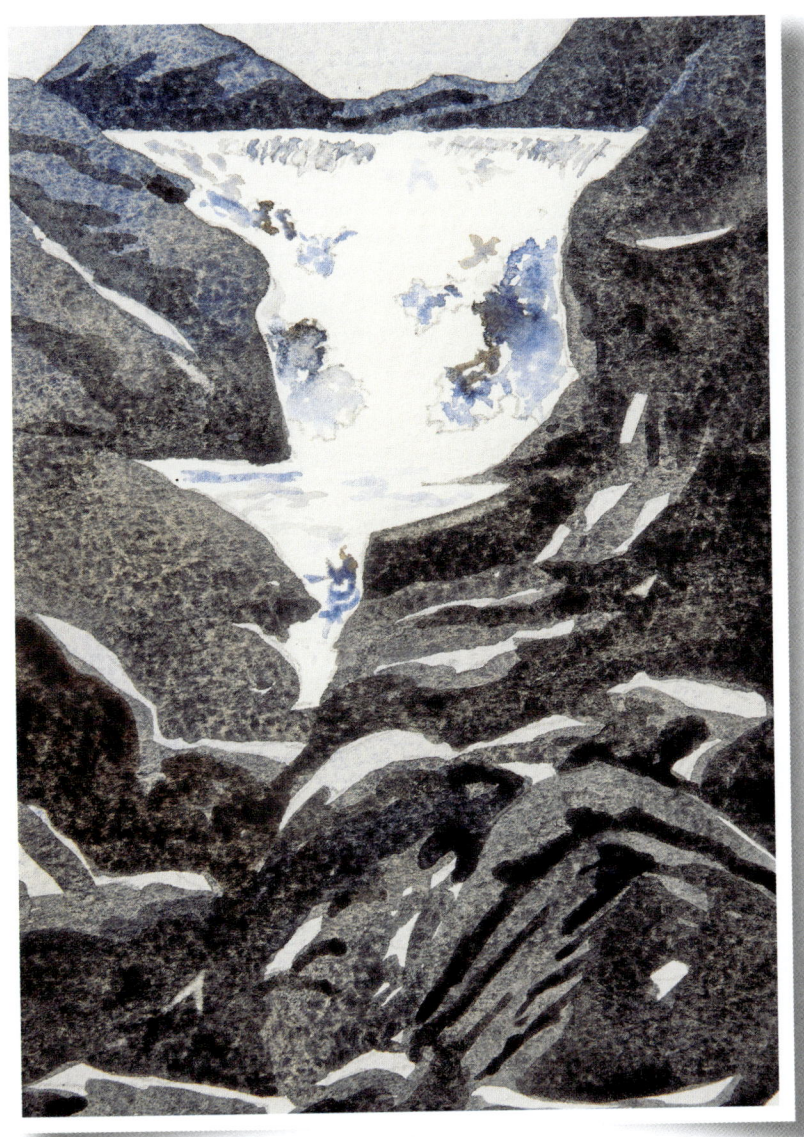

The finished postcard

Rock Textures

Here we have rocks of all sizes; a huge mountain in the distance, the cliff, then rocks and pebbles and foreground. Colours and detail are used to create that feeling of distance. This project is all about creating rocky effects, rather than attempting to paint every pebble.

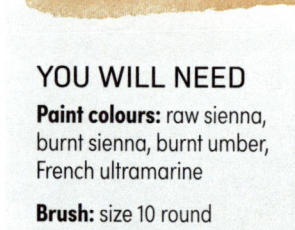

YOU WILL NEED

Paint colours: raw sienna, burnt sienna, burnt umber, French ultramarine

Brush: size 10 round

Other: outline drawing on page 88 (top)

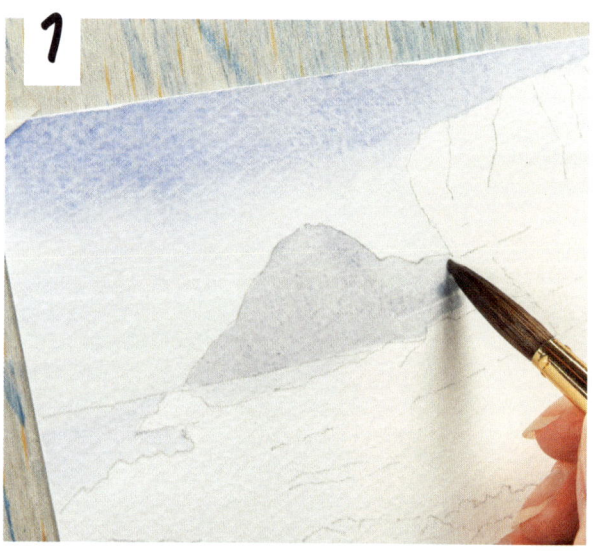

▶ Using a pale grey-blue mixture of French ultramarine and burnt umber, paint the sky, distant mountain, and sea. When dry, paint the mountain again with a similar mix.

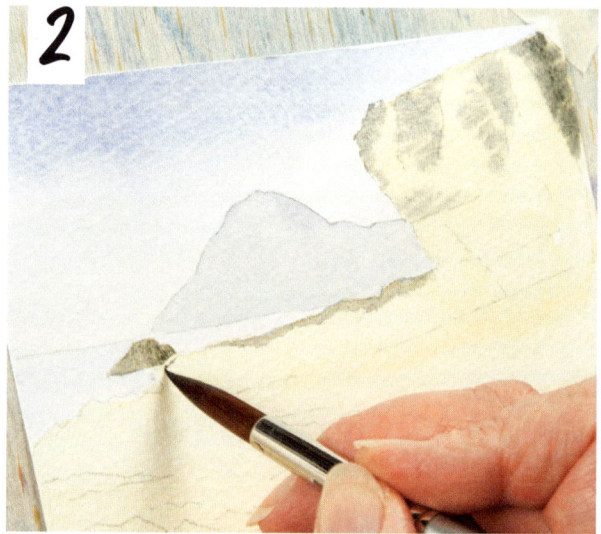

▶ Wash over all the rocks, cliff and beach with very pale raw sienna. Drop in the French ultramarine and burnt umber mix over the darker areas of the cliff and the rocks across the centre of the painting.

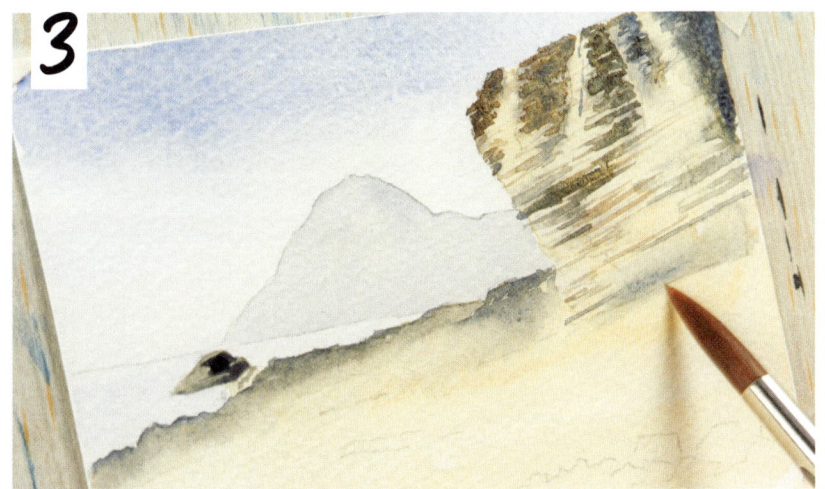

▶ Paint the distant rocks on the beach with the same mix, then the shadows and strata lines in the cliff face (using the point of your brush and a little paint in order to retain the point). Soften a few edges, and vary the proportions of the colours you use.

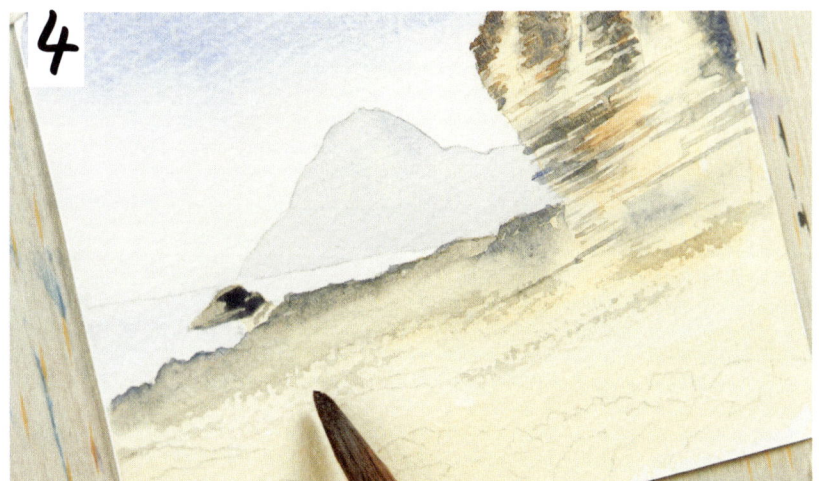

▶ Dry brush French ultramarine and burnt umber over the middle-distance area of the beach to suggest a few pebbles.

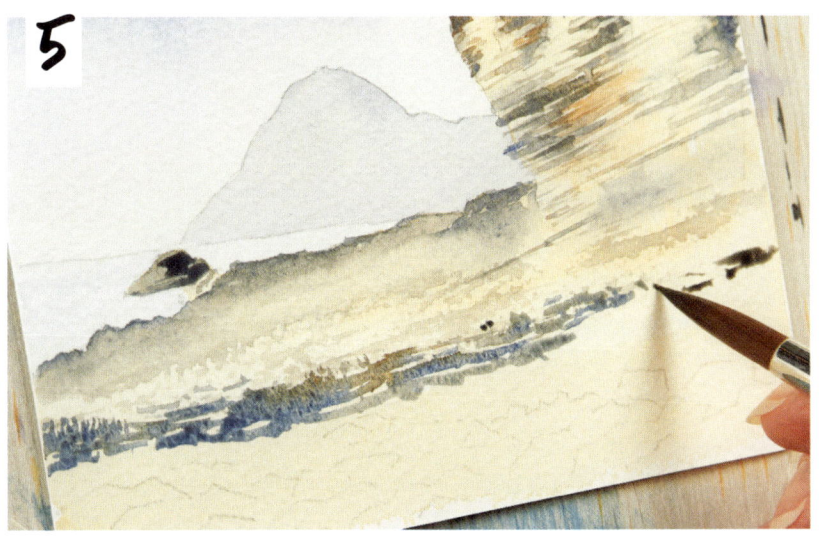

▶ Paint the foreground rocks with a strong mix of French ultramarine and burnt umber, beginning with loose dots and squiggles.

6

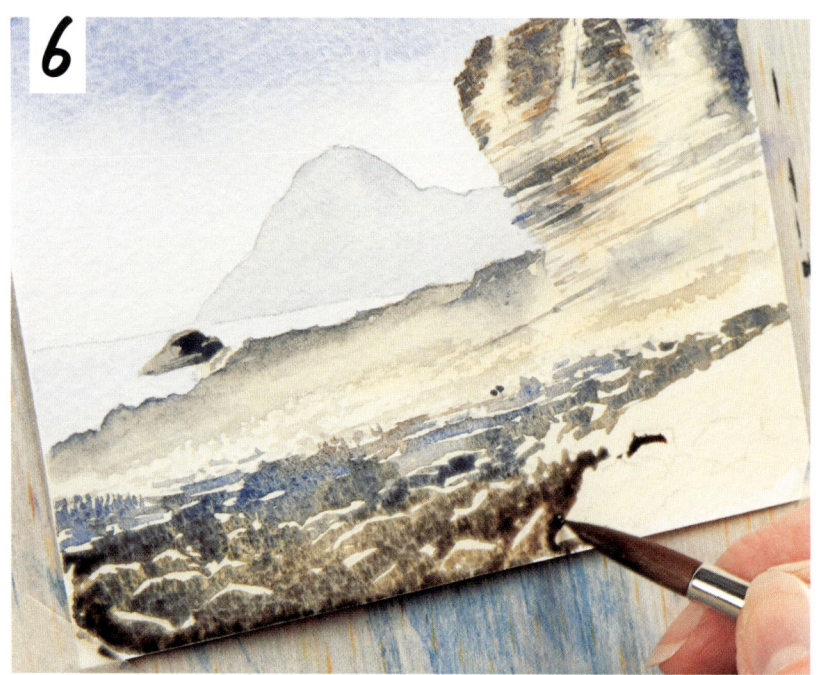

▶ Make the colour a little stronger and more biased towards brown as you come forward into the larger rocks; keep the paint wet so that each rock merges with the next. Leave highlights unpainted to define the tops of the rocks.

7

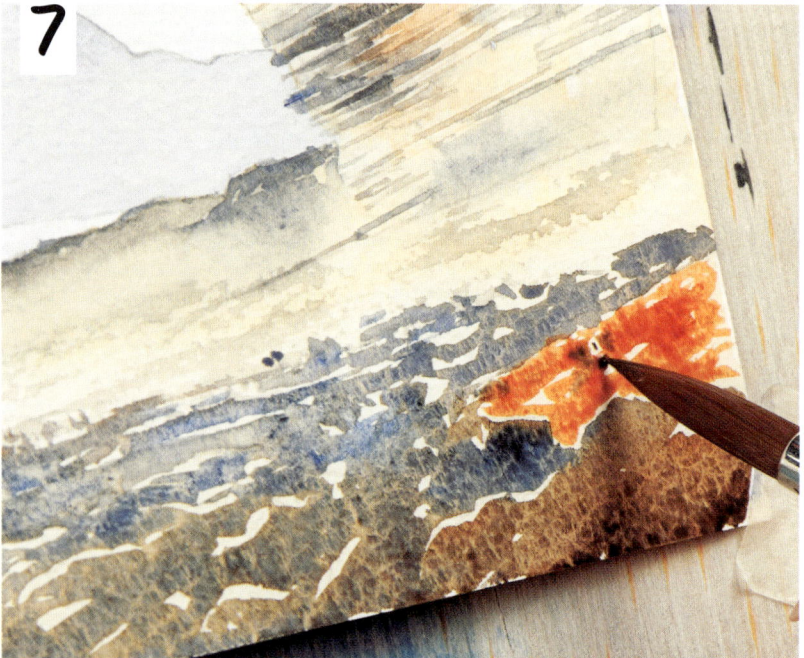

▶ Using a little burnt sienna paint the seaweed on the beach.

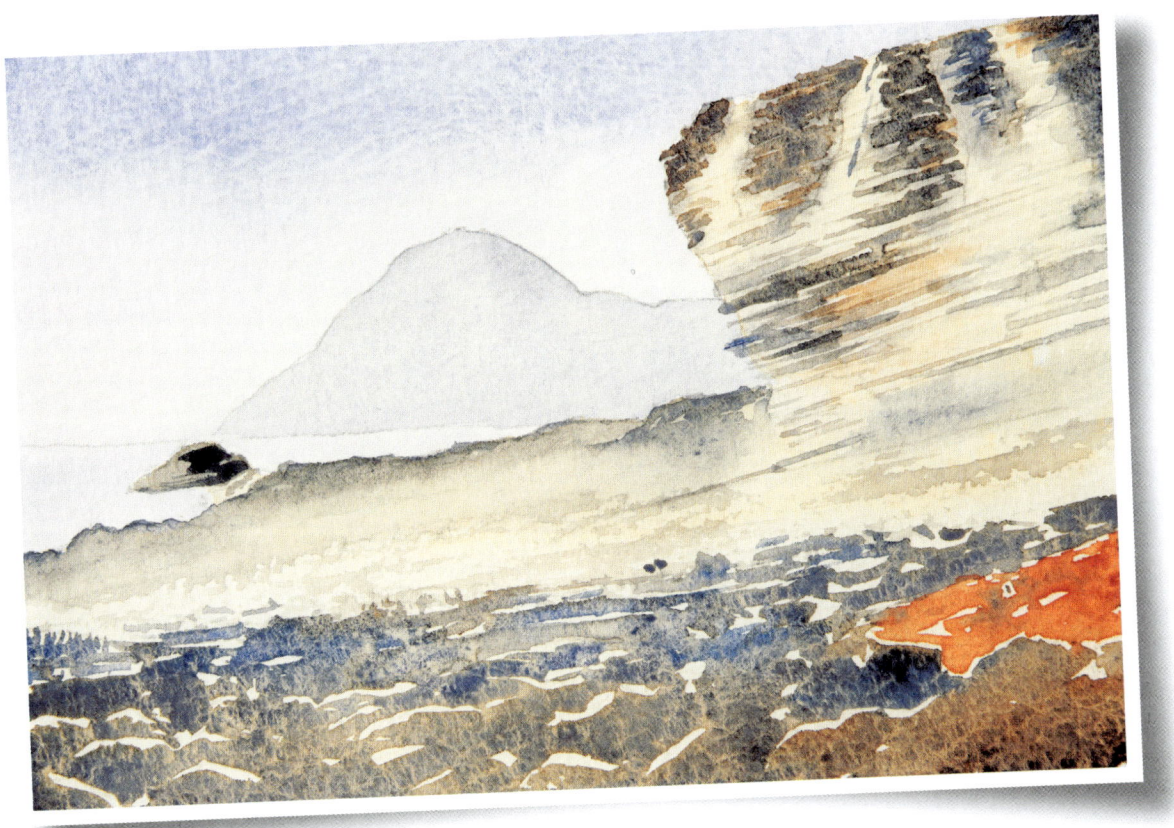

The finished postcard

Sunlight and Shadows

Shadows are created when something blocks a light source; they always fall away from that light. Their length, shape and sharpness changes according to the distance between the light and the object, and the angle of the light. Low winter sun creates long shadows, for example, while noon on a summer's day will be almost free of shadow. Shadows reveal contours and add tonal interest to a scene.

This scene is a stark contrast of warm oranges and cool shadows cast by the low sun and tall hills. Here, clouds and mountains interrupt light from the late evening sun, which illuminates the autumn vegetation on the nearer hill and gives it the strong colour.

YOU WILL NEED

Paint colours: Winsor yellow, permanent rose, burnt sienna, burnt umber, French ultramarine, cobalt blue

Brush: size 10 round

Other: outline drawing on page 88 (bottom)

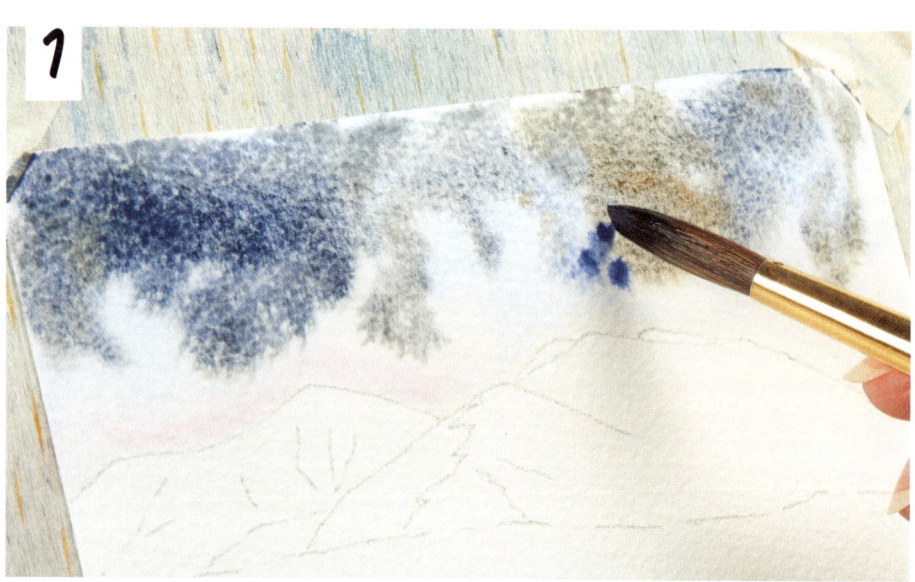

▶ Wet the sky area, drop in pale cobalt blue for most of the sky with very pale permanent rose below. While this is still damp, drop in clouds of a French ultramarine and burnt umber mix.

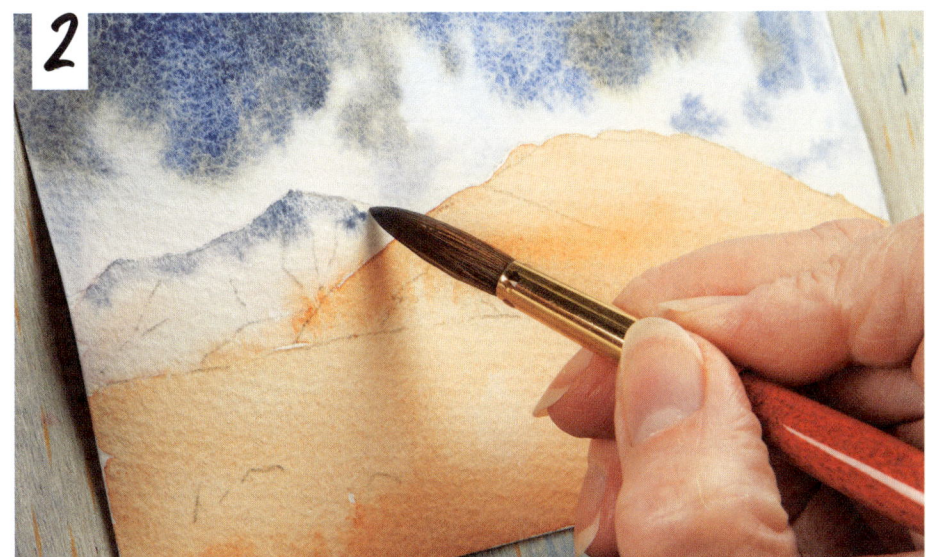

▶ Paint the hills – pale permanent rose and a little burnt sienna for the hill on the left and burnt sienna for the hill on the right; allow the two hills to merge together. Continue with burnt sienna for the moorland, then drop in a French ultramarine and burnt umber mix to the top of the hill on the left for the cloud shadow.

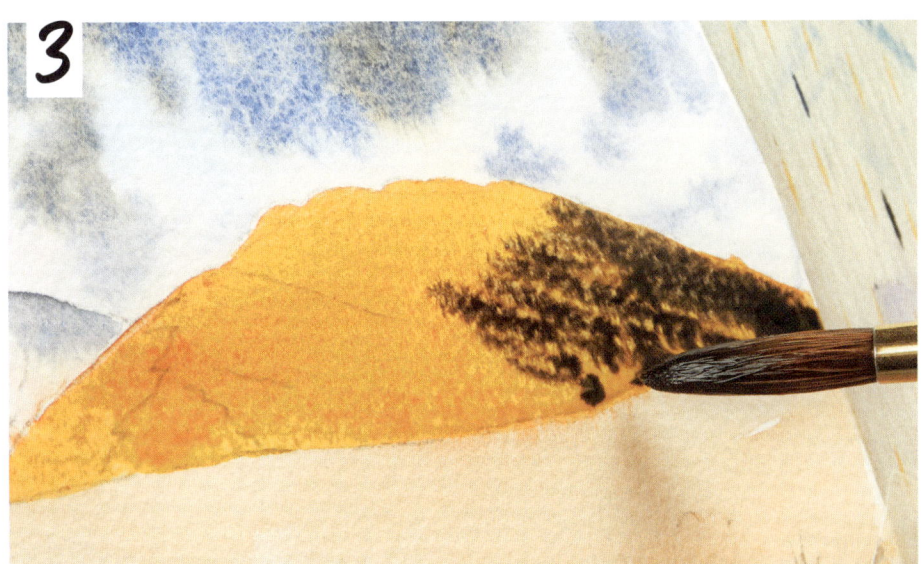

▶ Re-wet the hill on the right and drop in burnt sienna and Winsor yellow. When this is damp, paint the cloud shadow with a stronger mix of French ultramarine and burnt umber, making diagonal movements with the brush. The dampness of the paper should give you slightly blurred, soft edges.

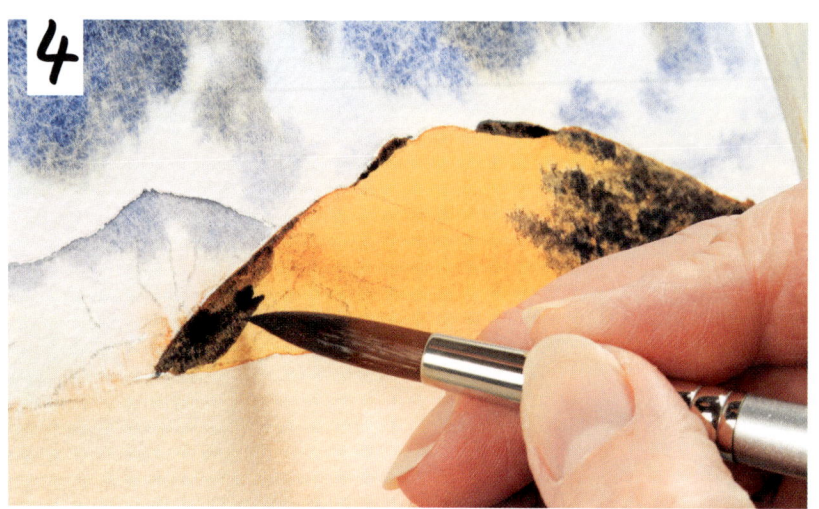

▶ Paint the top of the hill on the right and the shadow to the left of this hill using the French ultramarine and burnt umber mix. Aim to create crisp edges by using the point of the brush.

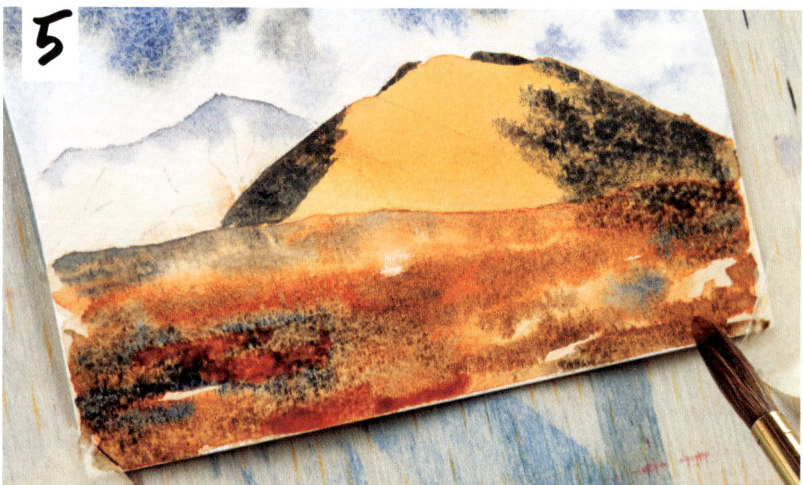

▶ Re-wet, roughly, the moorland (it does not matter if some areas remain dry). Paint some stronger darks to add a little texture to the foreground, using burnt sienna and the French ultramarine and burnt umber mix added wet into wet.

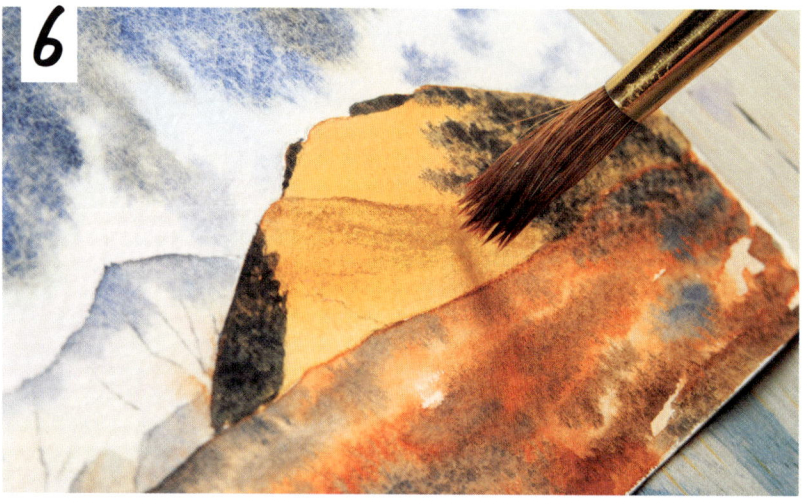

▶ Add detail to the hills and foreground with a dilute mix of burnt umber and French ultramarine, applying the paint with a split brush (see page 22).

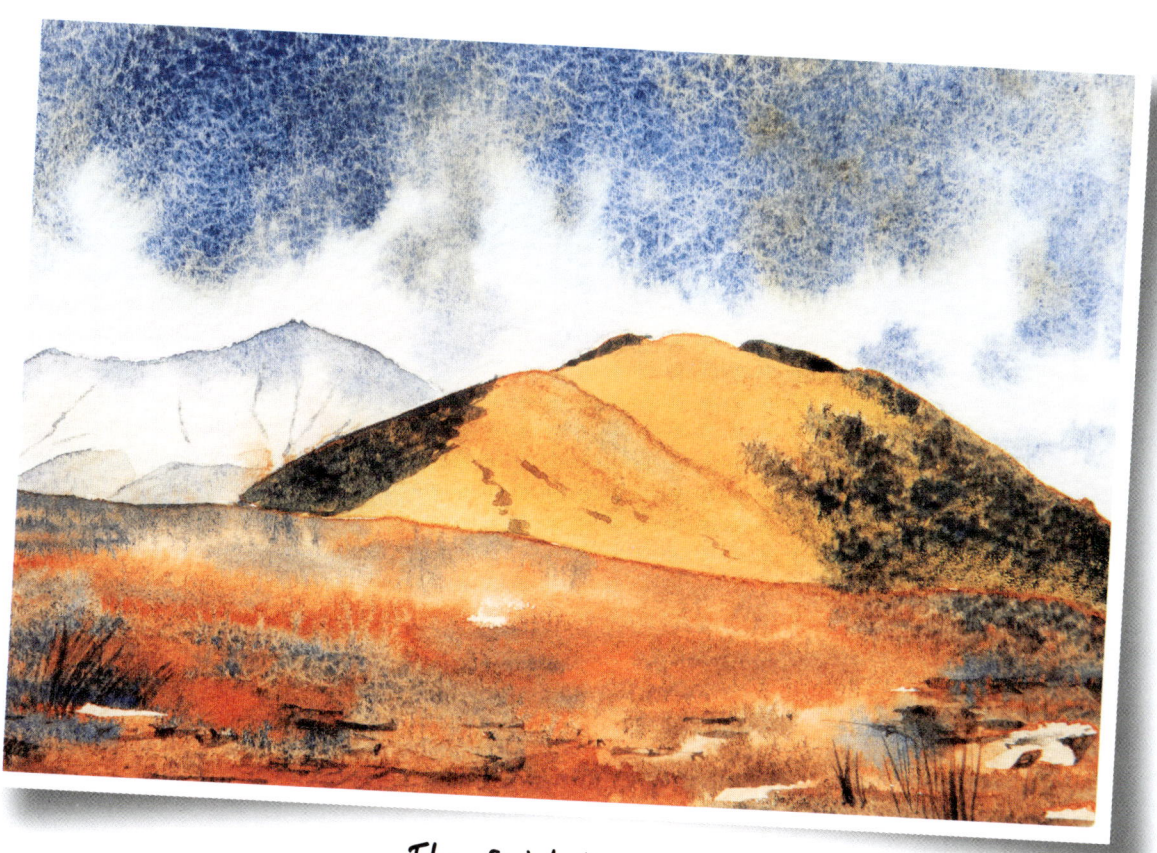

The finished postcard

Reflections

Still water is occasionally seen as 'still as a millpond' and this gives crisp mirrored reflections, but it often has a slight shimmer when ruffled by a gentle breeze; that's what we'll look at here.

While getting used to the wet into wet technique you might find it useful to paint reflections before the subject that's actually making them; that way if your reflection goes a little astray you can adjust the position of the subject to match it.

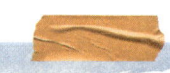

YOU WILL NEED

Paint colours: French ultramarine, burnt umber, raw sienna, permanent rose

Brush: size 10 round

Other: outline drawing on page 89

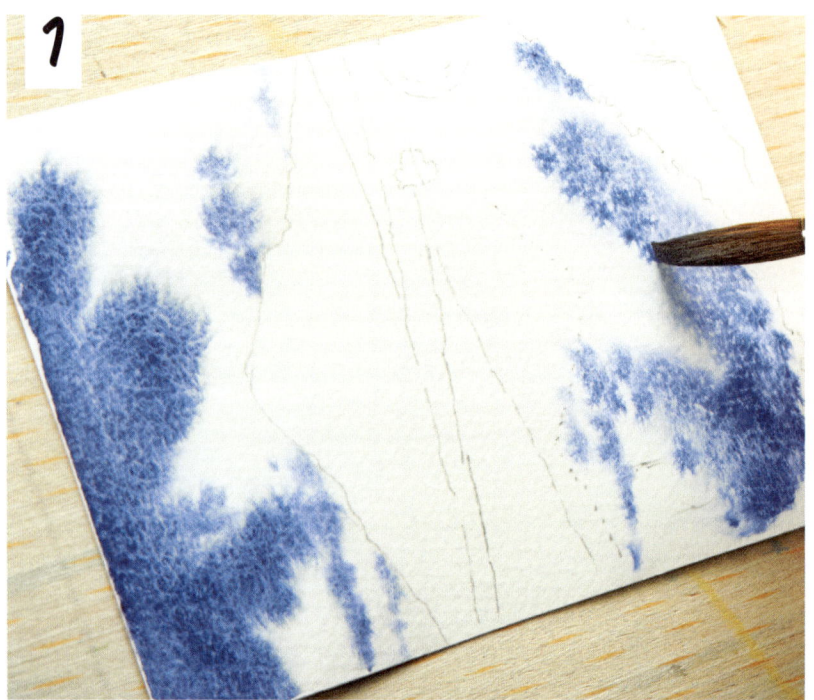

▶ Wet the sky area and drop in clouds with a French ultramarine and burnt umber mix. Dampen the pool area and drop in reflections to loosely mirror the clouds, hill and rocks as shown. Allow to dry.

Painting reflections

When painting reflections, you may find it helpful to turn your painting on its side, as shown here. This makes it easier to check the symmetry.

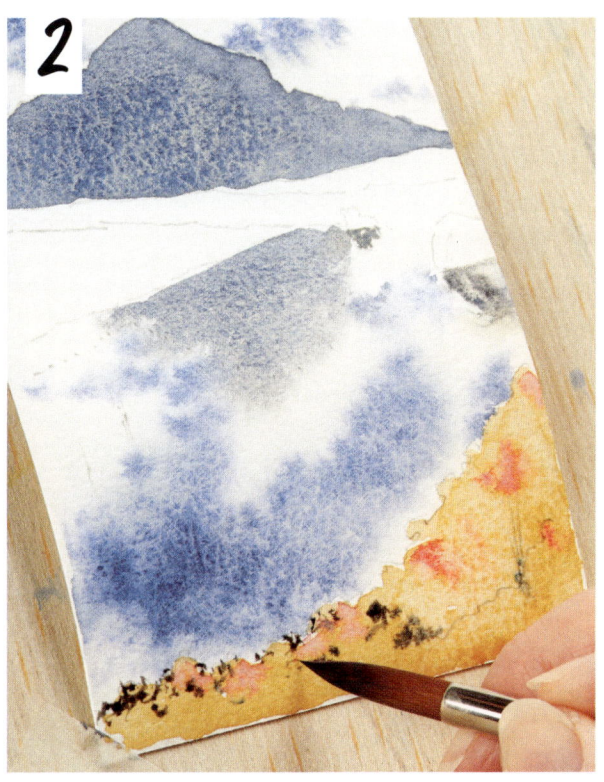

2

▶ Use the French ultramarine and burnt umber mix to paint the main mountains. Paint the golds of the moorland below the pool with raw sienna. While wet, drop in permanent rose, then the French ultramarine and burnt umber mix to darken the area.

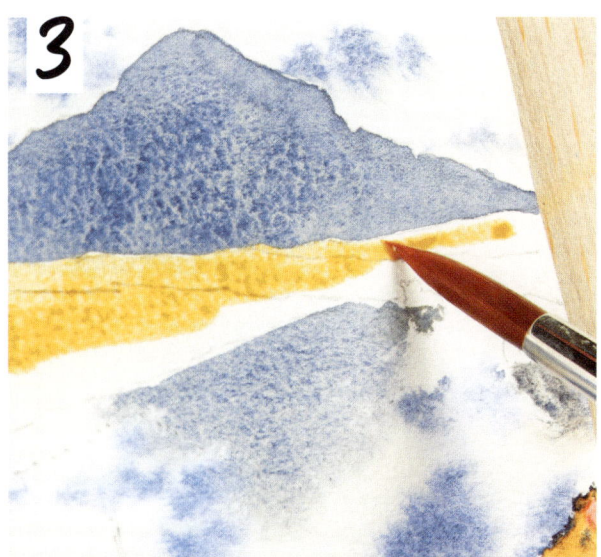

3

▶ Paint the golden moorland between the pool and the hills using raw sienna.

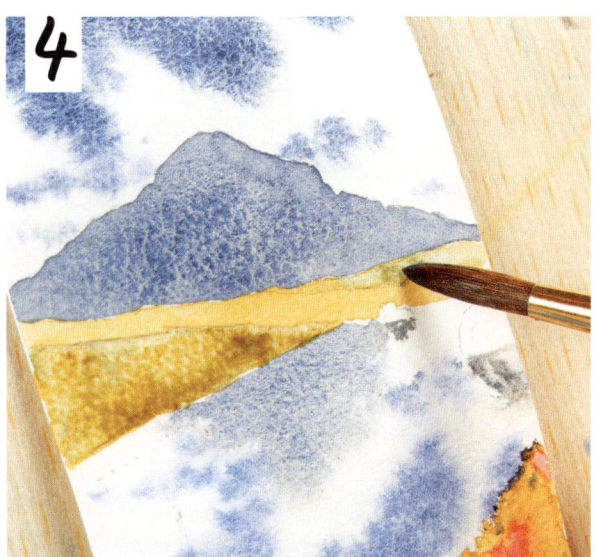

4

▶ Using a French ultramarine and raw sienna mix, paint over the gold areas to create a soft green.

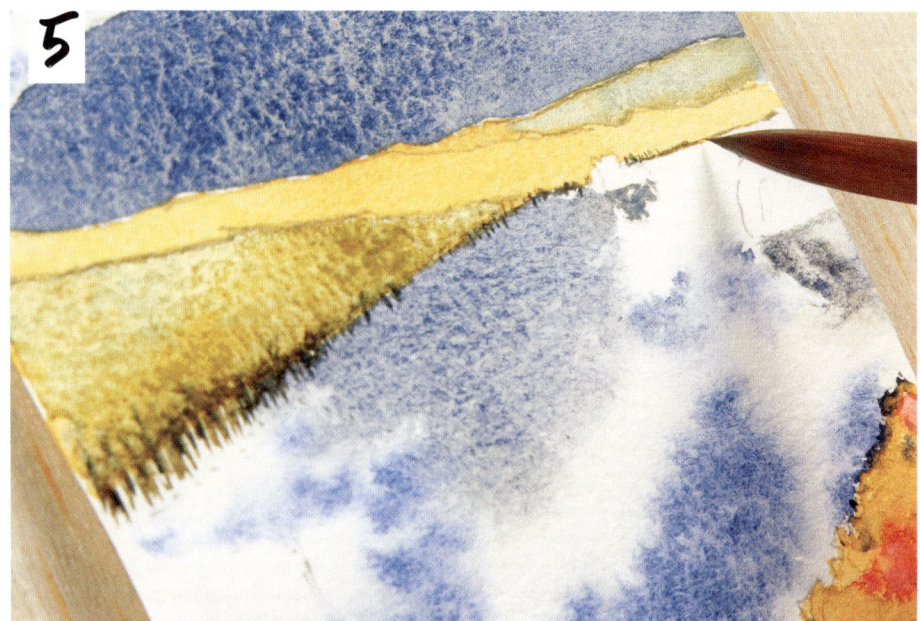

▶ Drop in a darker mix of the same colours near the water's edge and paint the reflections of the grass, then paint the water's edge to the right of the rock.

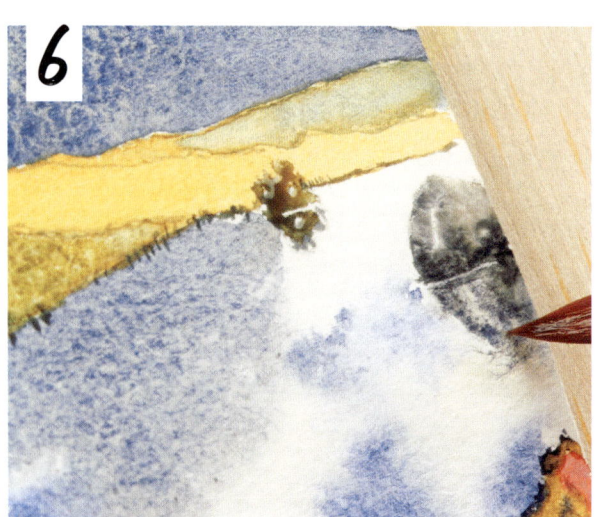

▶ Paint the rocks in the pool with a combination of two mixes: French ultramarine and burnt umber, and French ultramarine and raw sienna.

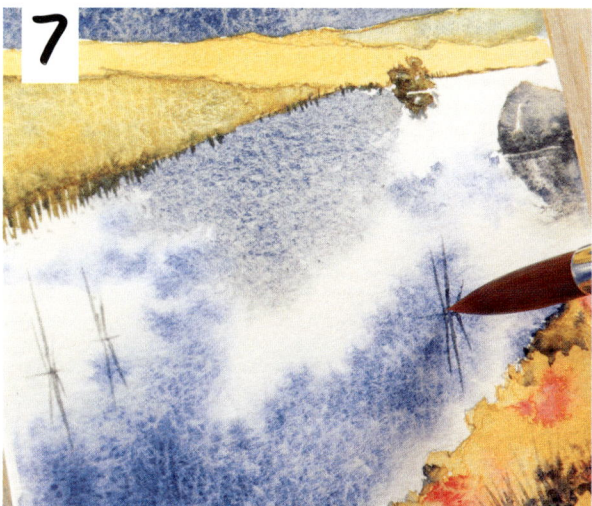

▶ Paint a few grasses in the foreground and in the pool. If necessary, slightly sharpen the reflection of the hill with a pale mix of the hill colours to finish.

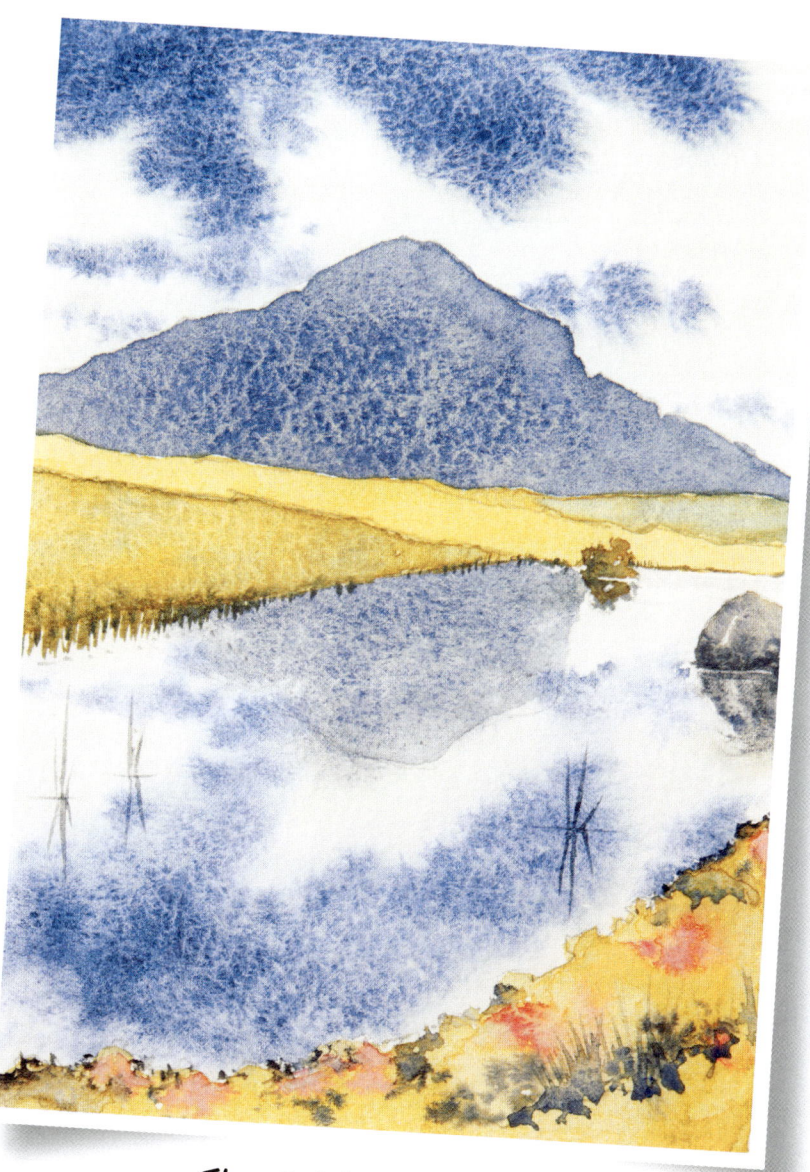

The finished postcard

Mountain and Sea

Making water look wet: sometimes less really is more. The less you do to create an effect, the more effective the result. This project shows you how to create the impression of a thin layer of water over the beach. We paint the wash that represents the water over a dry wash that represents the beach; the sand then naturally shows through the water, just as in life.

The outline includes some fine details of wave crests and distant sails. Don't despair if you accidentally paint over these at step 3; carry on, then try again with a new outline when you have time. Alternatively, you could cut slivers of masking tape to reserve the white of the paper for the sails, removing them when the painting is completely dry.

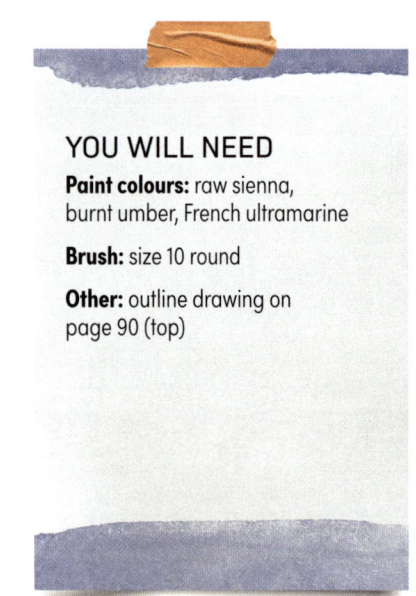

YOU WILL NEED

Paint colours: raw sienna, burnt umber, French ultramarine

Brush: size 10 round

Other: outline drawing on page 90 (top)

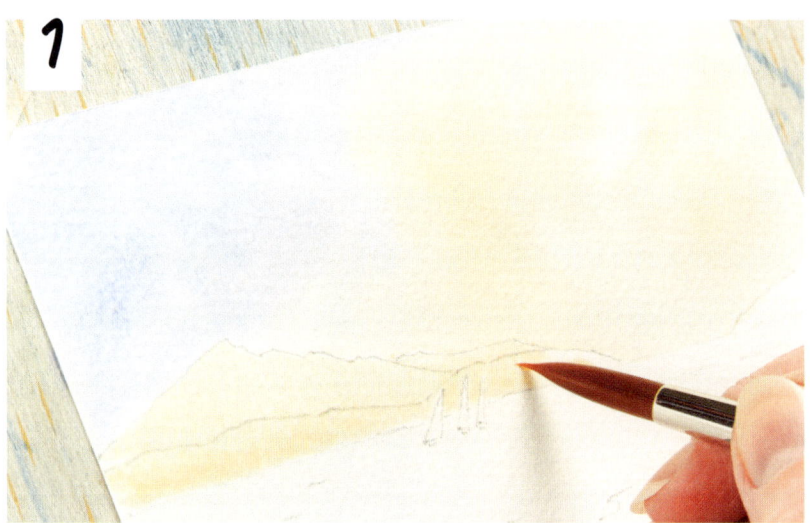

▶ Wet the sky. Drop in very pale raw sienna to the centre and right, and French ultramarine to the left. Paint the distant mountains (on the left) with the same pale raw sienna.

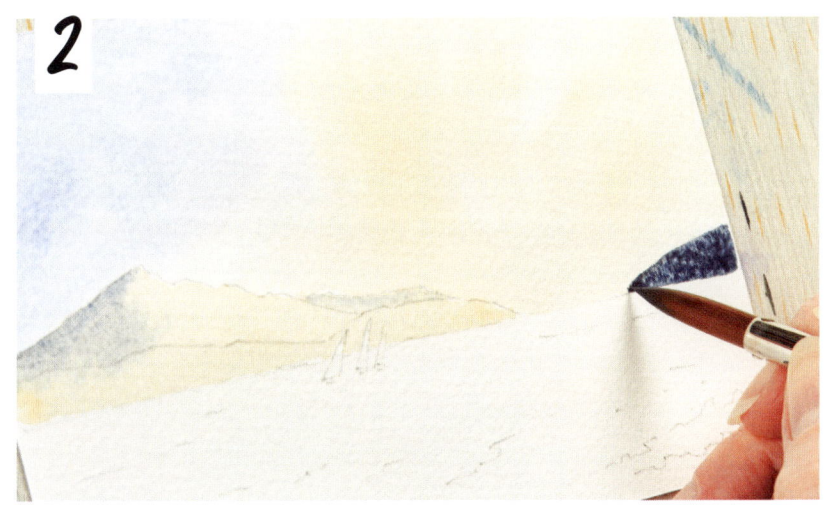

▶ While the distant mountains are wet, drop in a pale mix of French ultramarine and burnt umber. Paint the hills on the right with a stronger mix of the same colours.

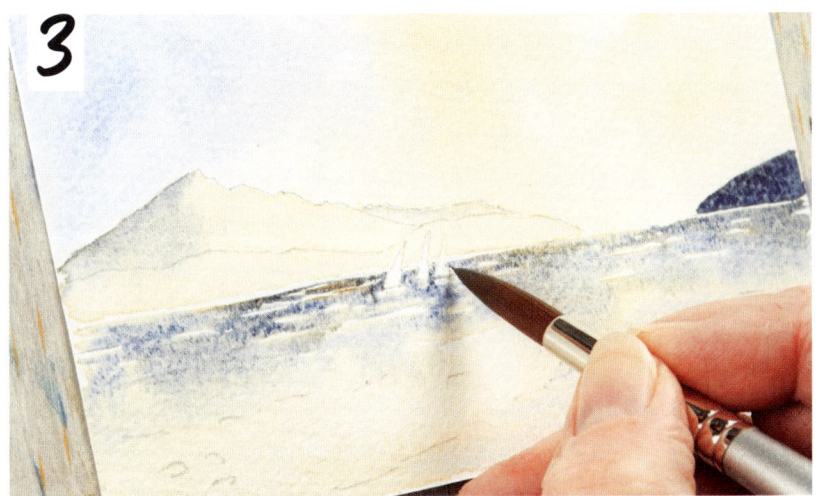

▶ Paint the sea and beach with pale raw sienna, leaving the sail shapes and a few small horizontal bands of paper – for waves – unpainted. Drop in the French ultramarine and burnt umber mix to the sea, particularly further away, towards the horizon.

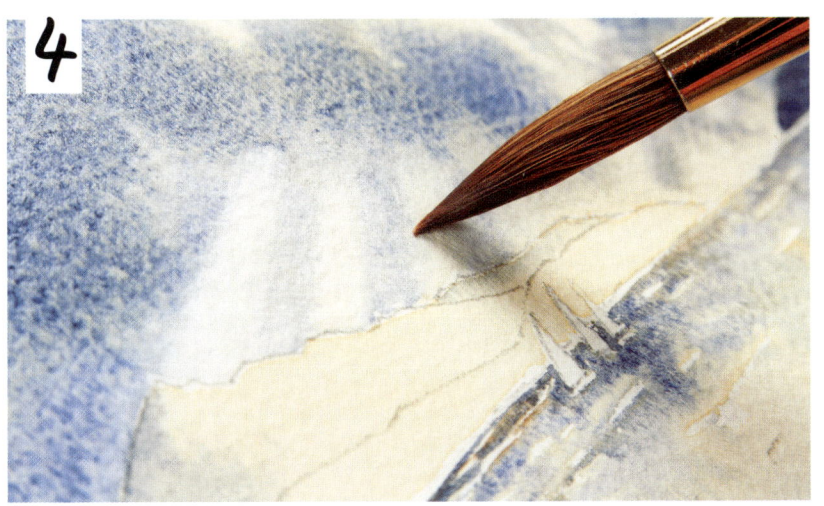

▶ Re-wet the sky and paint the storm cloud with a stronger mix of French ultramarine and burnt umber. Create a few sunbeams while the paper is still damp (these should radiate from the light area of sky); lift out and add colour as necessary while the paint is still damp. Try not to overwork these, we need only to suggest the light.

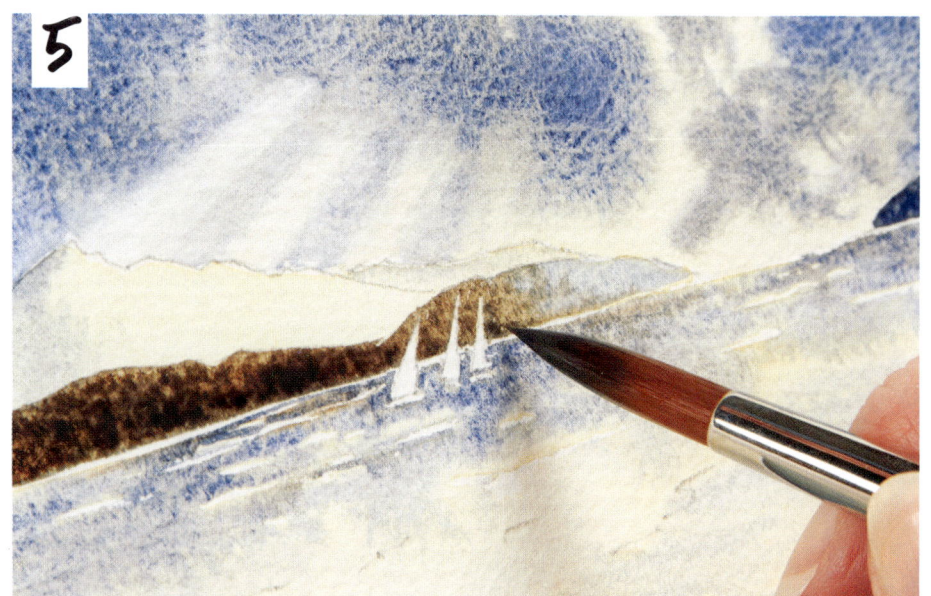

5

▶ Add a little more burnt umber to the French ultramarine and burnt umber mix for the foremost land mass. Use a pale blue mix where it is more distant.

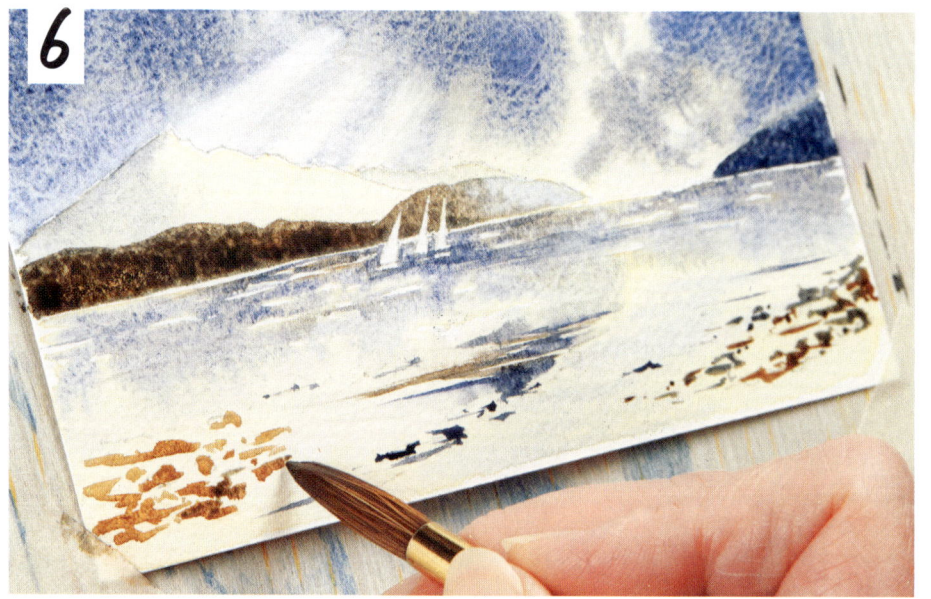

6

▶ Mix various combinations of French ultramarine and burnt umber, making some more blue, some more brown, and in varied strengths (i.e. with more or less water), paint dots and broken strokes/dry brush for the stones and detail on the beach.

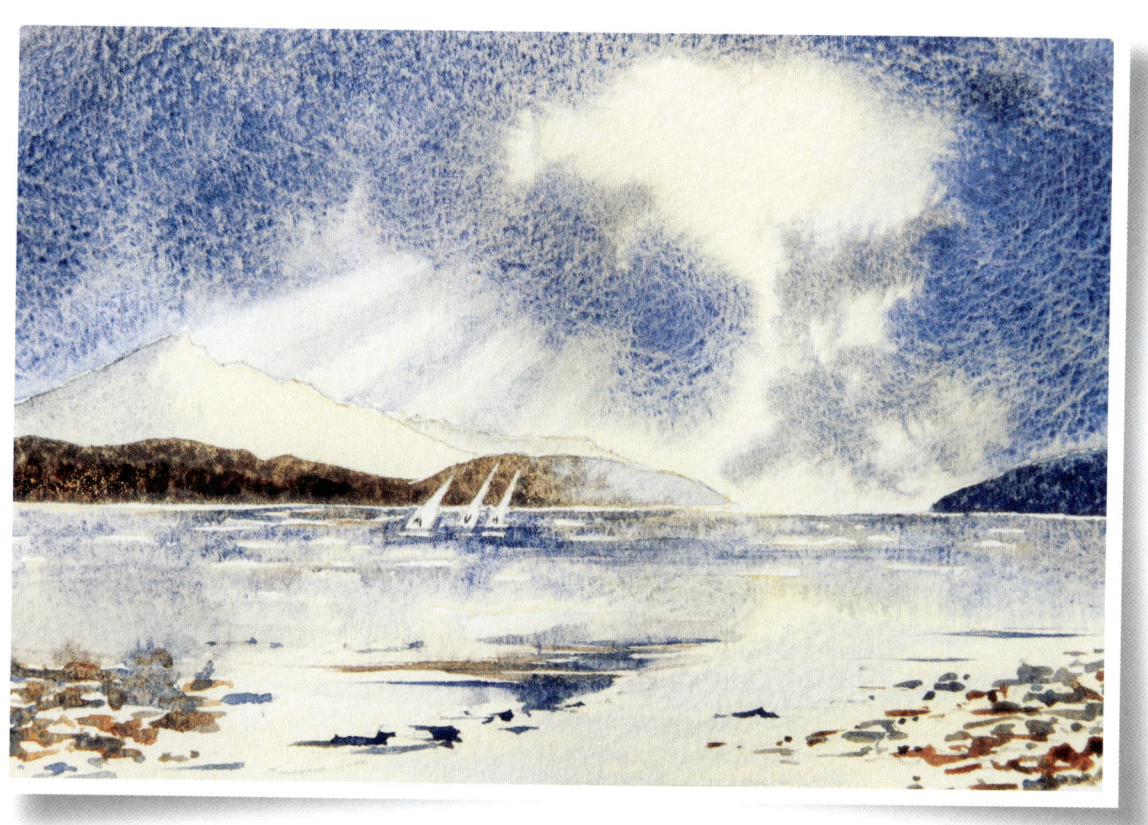

The finished postcard

Wavelets and Ripples

When painting wavelets and ripples it's important to look at the shapes that actually occur rather than guessing or rushing to complete the work and painting a sea of worms or small fish. Wavelets and ripples need to be fluid and smooth: a combination of hard and soft edges may make them more convincing. Try to convey perspective in the size of the waves you paint; larger in the foreground, smaller in the distance.

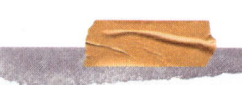

YOU WILL NEED

Paint colours: French ultramarine, raw sienna, burnt sienna, permanent rose

Brush: size 10 round

Other: outline drawing on page 90 (bottom)

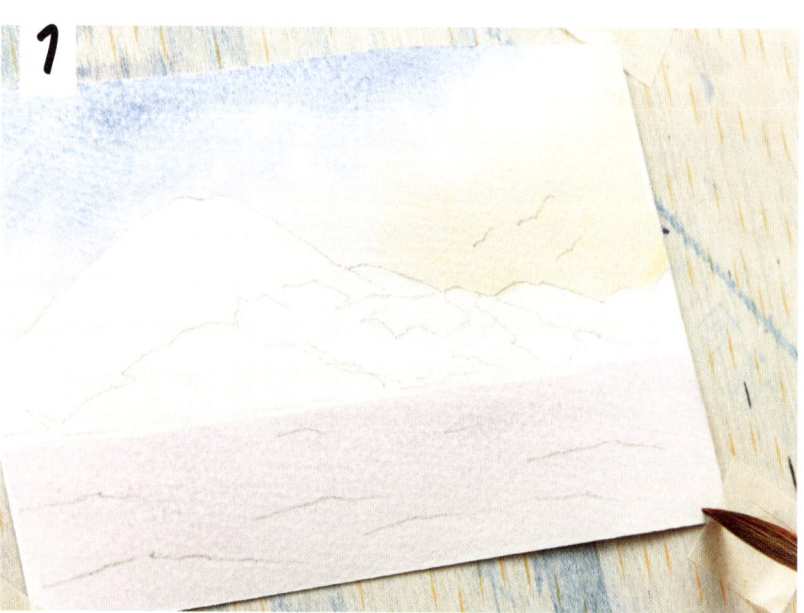

► Wet the sky area. Drop in French ultramarine to the top, and raw sienna to the lower right sky. Use a light, dull purple mix of French ultramarine, burnt sienna and permanent rose to paint the sea, leaving a fine line of clean dry paper below the land mass.

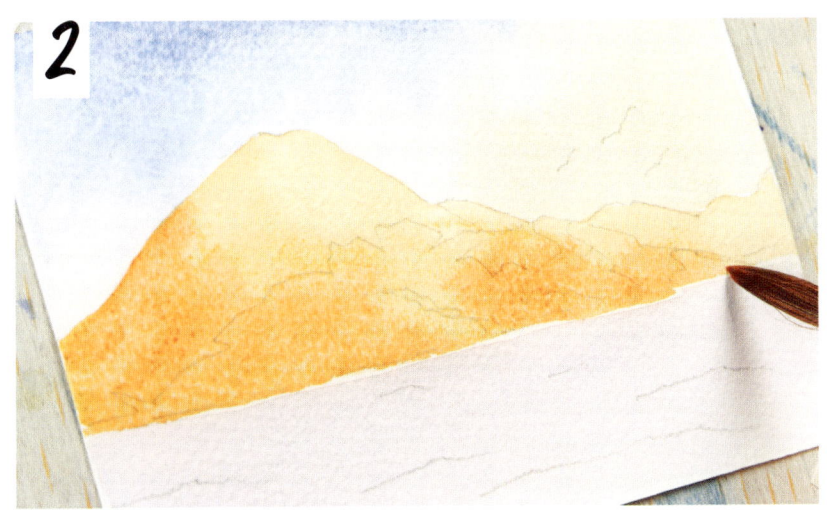

▶ Paint raw sienna on to the hills, adding a little burnt sienna to the mix for the lower slopes.

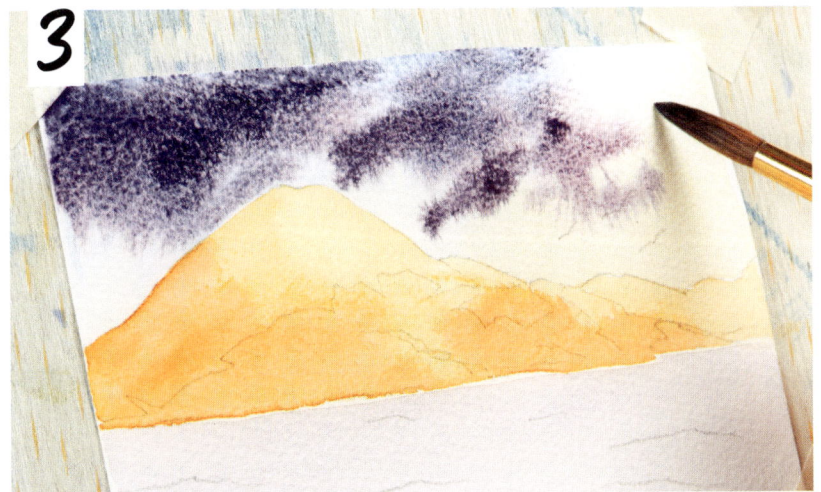

▶ Re-wet the sky and add storm clouds of a French ultramarine, burnt sienna and permanent rose mix.

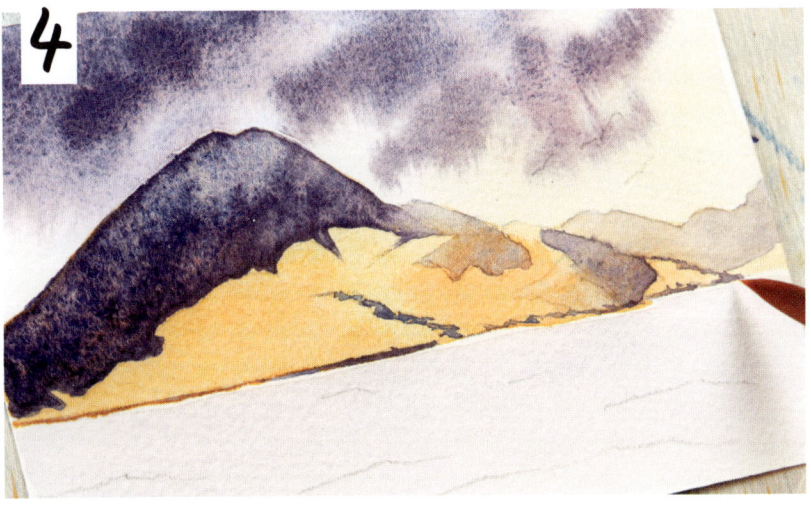

▶ Paint a French ultramarine and permanent rose mix over the darker areas of the hill and the details at the shoreline.

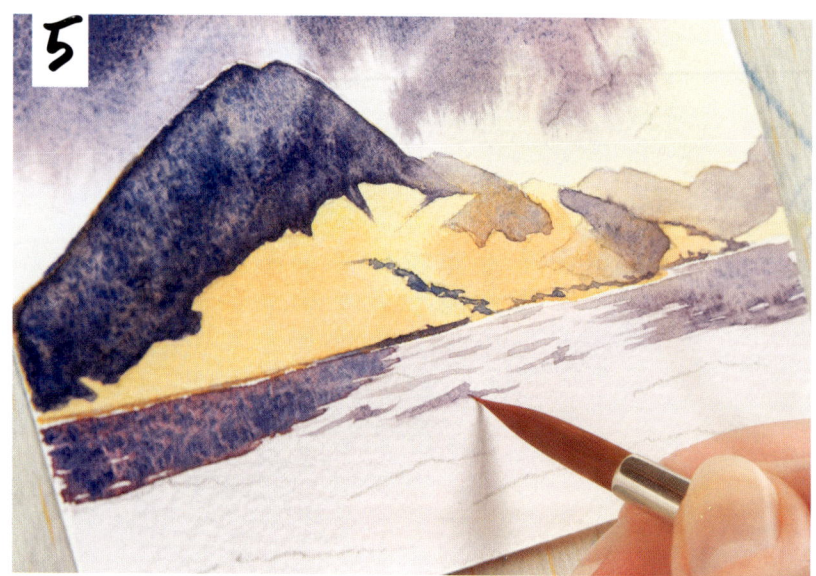

▶ Strengthen the tones in the sea; darkest on the left where the hill is dark, and paint waves – starting with small, pale, fine lines in the distance.

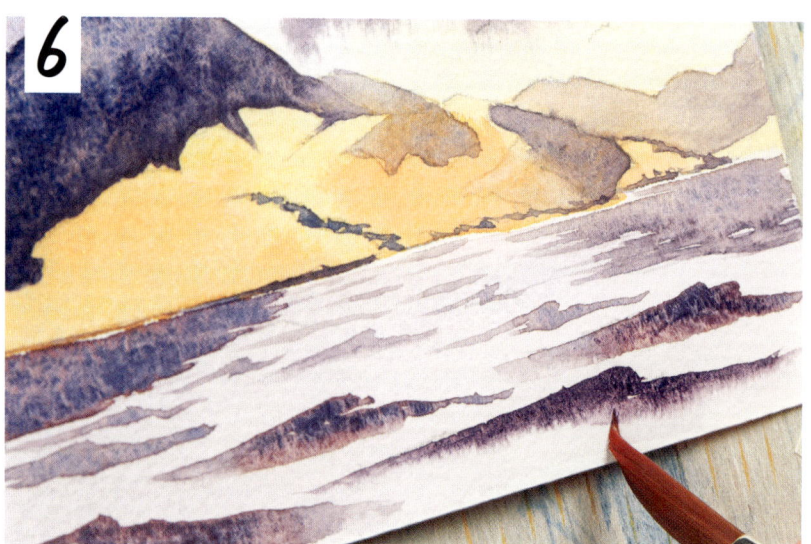

▶ Add larger, darker, more widely spaced waves in the foreground, using a fluid ripple stroke. Soften the lower edge of a few of the larger ripples with a clean damp brush.

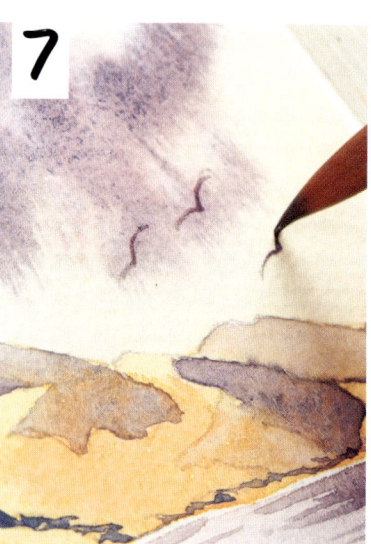

▶ With a little of the same paint mix on the point of your brush, add a few simple birds to finish.

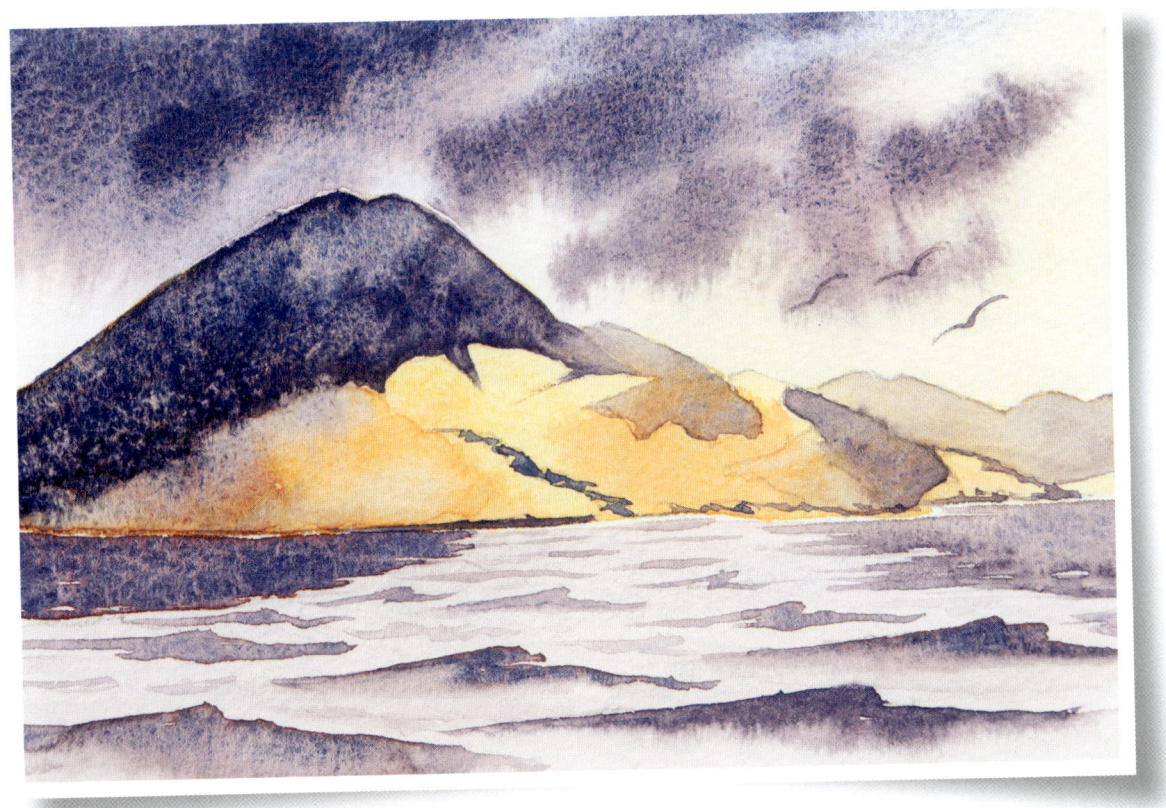

The finished postcard

Chill Peaks

Although the use of cool colours in a mountain painting will give a convincing chilly feel, it can also result in an unattractively cold finished postcard. Your painting can often be enhanced by introducing a little warm colour: adding a little warmth will create contrast and so emphasize the cold. By doing so, you can often make a more successful painting.

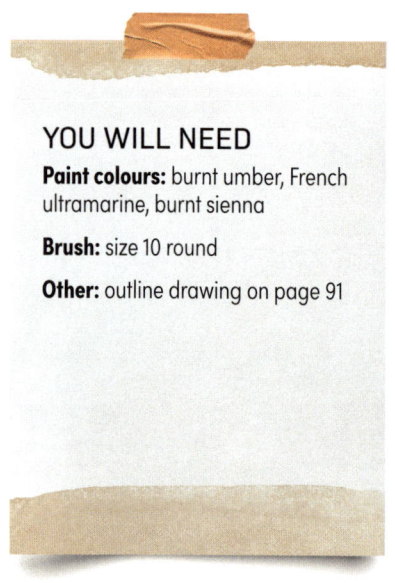

YOU WILL NEED

Paint colours: burnt umber, French ultramarine, burnt sienna

Brush: size 10 round

Other: outline drawing on page 91

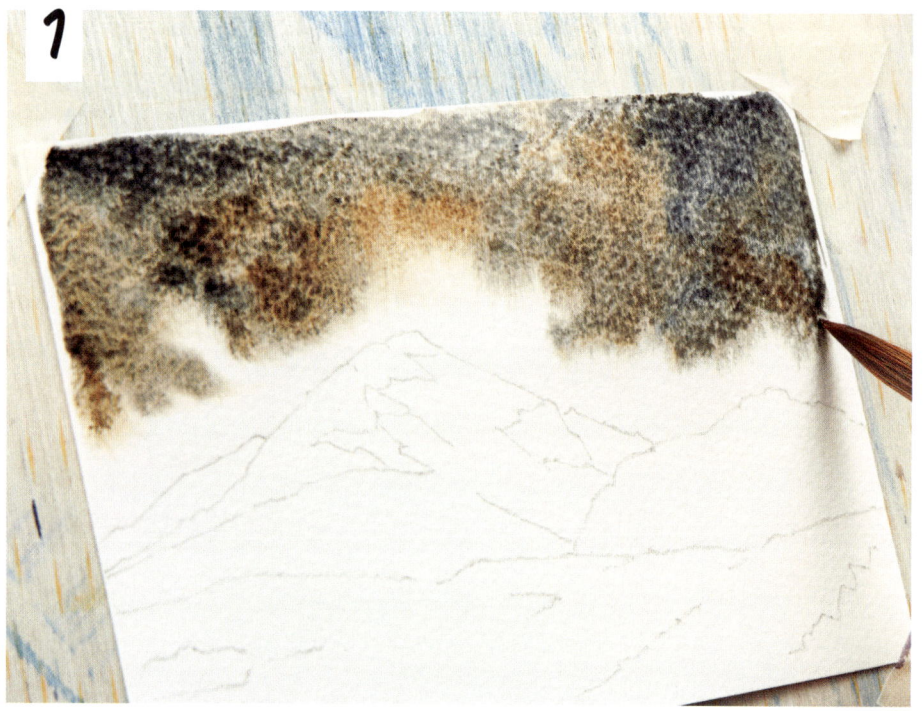

▶ Wet the sky area and drop in a mix of French ultramarine and burnt umber to represent clouds.

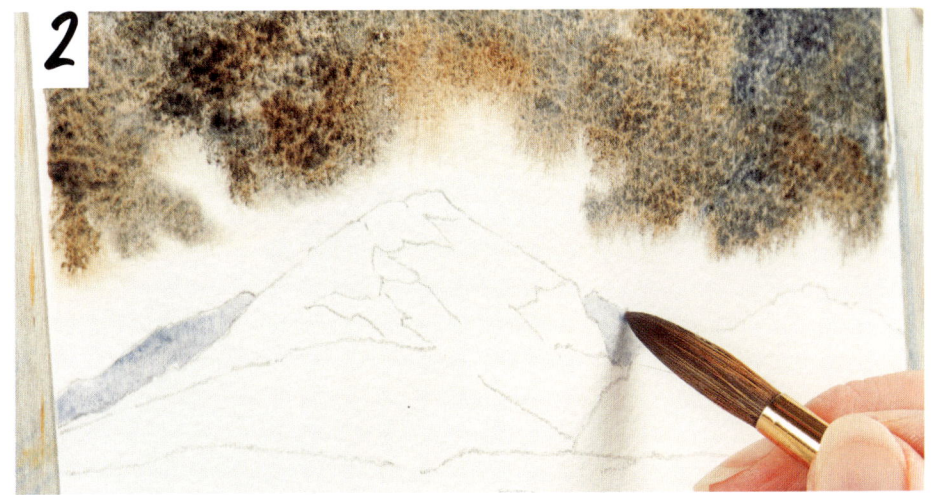

▶ Paint the small areas of background mountains (on either side of the main peak) with a grey-blue mix of French ultramarine and burnt umber.

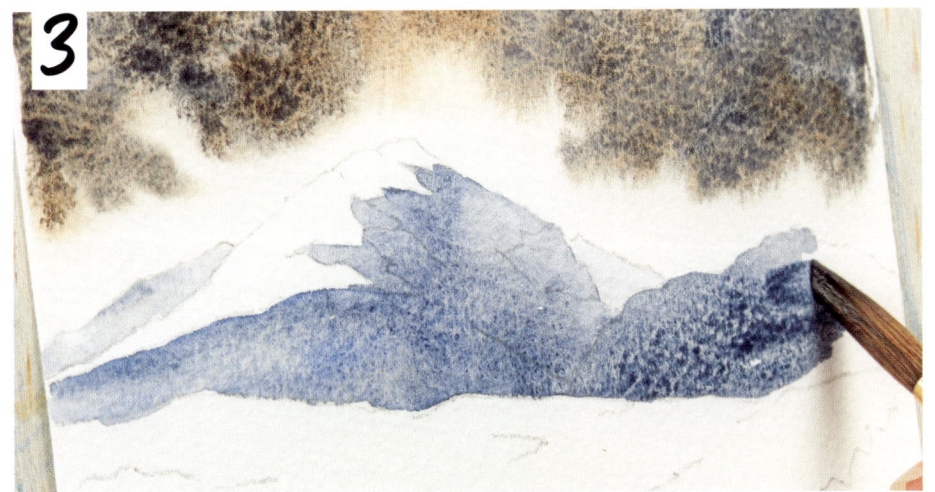

▶ With a stronger mix, more biased to blue, paint the main mountain and the hill to the right.

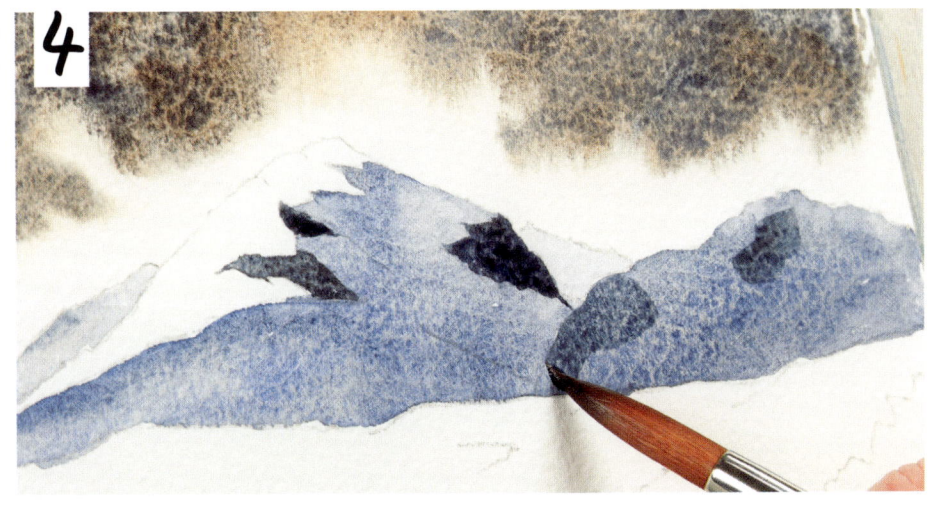

▶ Once completely dry, add darker tones to the mountains with glazes of the blue-biased mix.

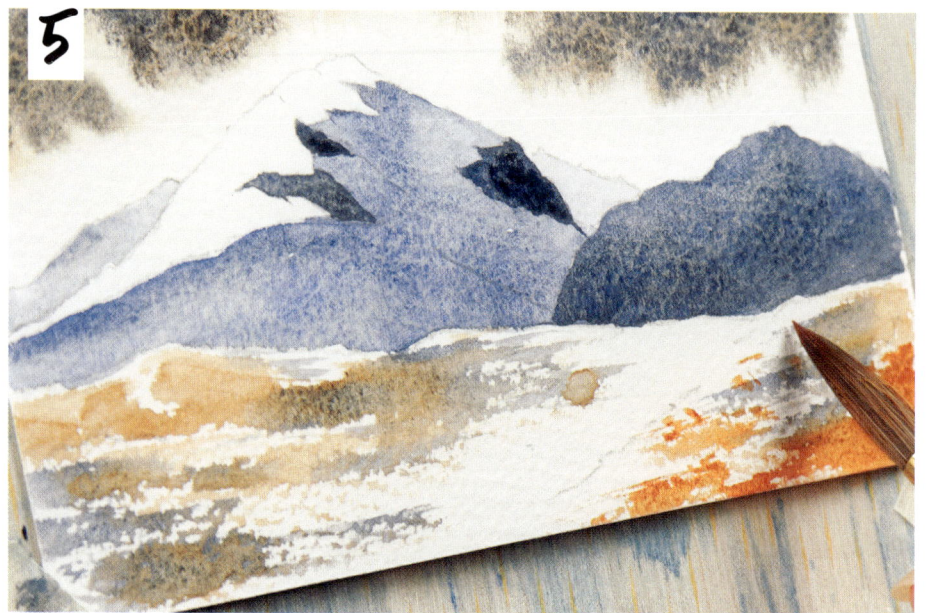

▶ Dry brush burnt umber over the foreground. While damp, paint strokes of burnt sienna and French ultramarine and burnt umber through it to soften here and there.

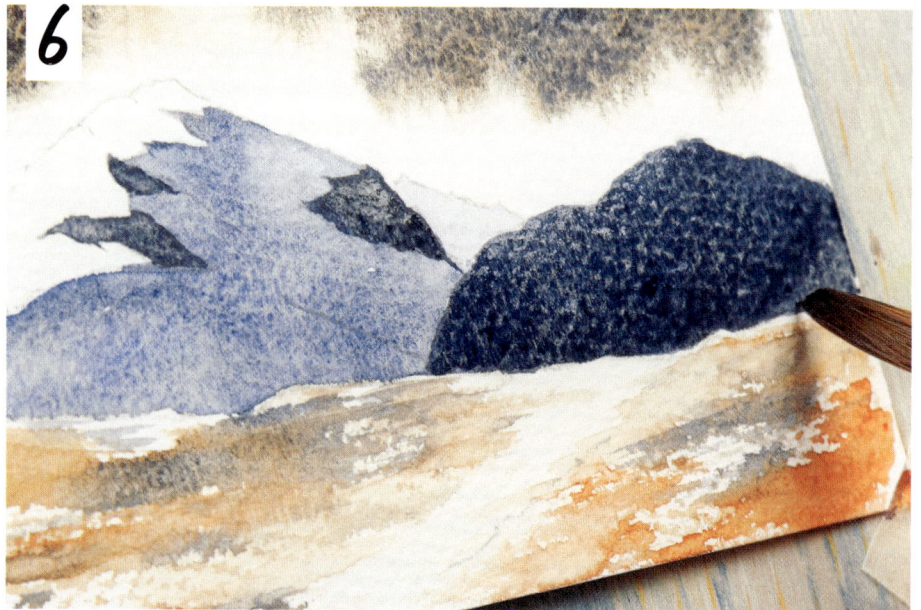

▶ Further strengthen the hill in shadow with the blue-biased French ultramarine and burnt umber mix.

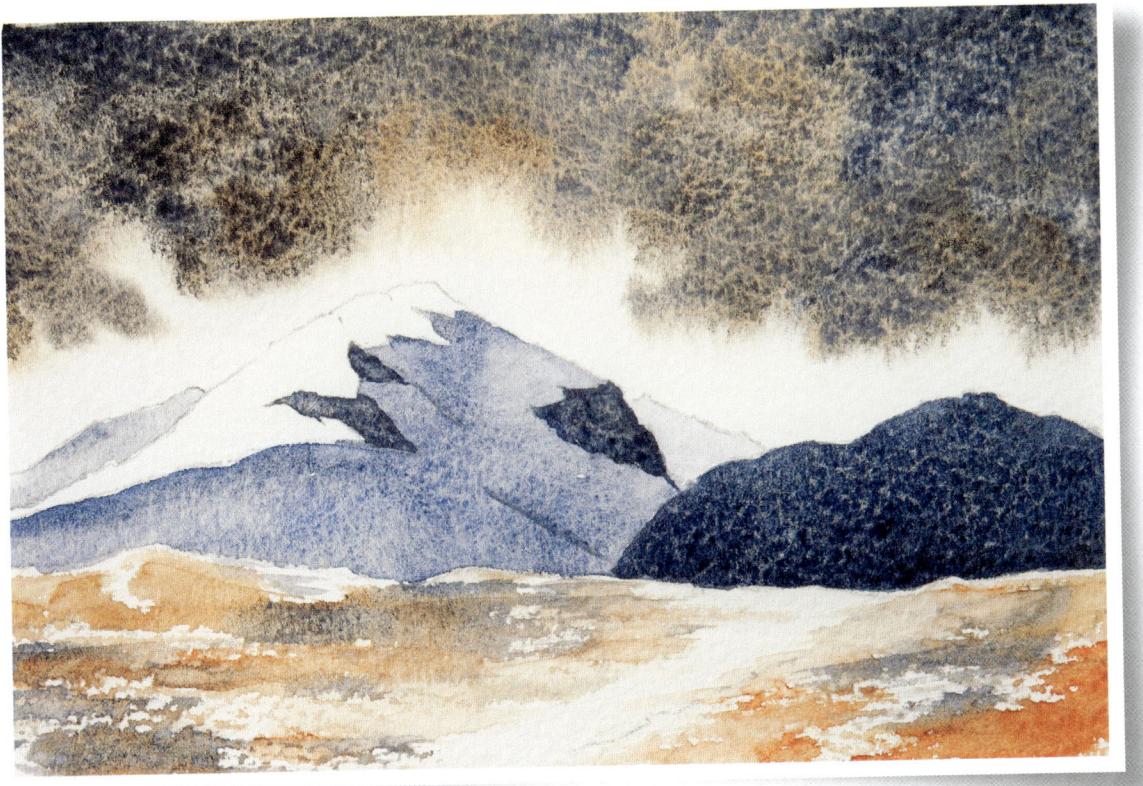

The finished postcard

Warming and cooling

Try this exercise again, this time using warmer or cooler colours and find out which approach gives you the result you wish for.

Snowy Summit

Sometimes it isn't enough to leave the paper showing through to give the white of snow, because the snow we need to portray appears softly golden in sunlight, greyed by shadow, or rosy in sunrise or sunset conditions. Contrasts of warm and cold will generally make a more interesting painting.

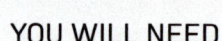

YOU WILL NEED

Paint colours: French ultramarine, burnt umber, raw sienna, Winsor yellow

Brush: size 10 round

Other: outline drawing on page 92

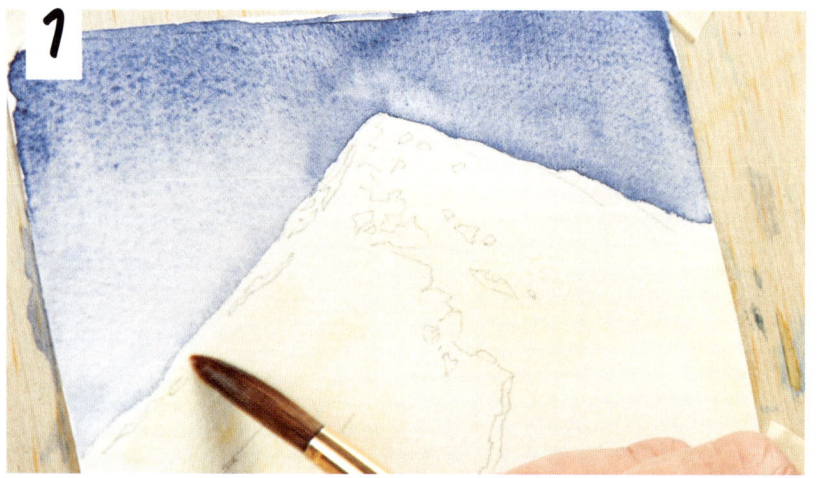

▶ Wash on French ultramarine and burnt umber mix to the sky, graduating it a little around the mountain. Once dry, paint a very pale wash of raw sienna and a tiny amount of Winsor yellow all over the mountain.

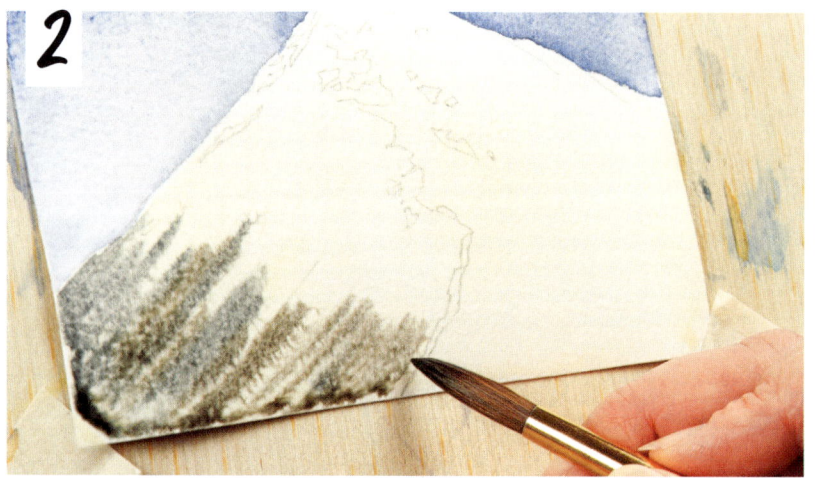

▶ While the mountain is still damp, paint a French ultramarine and burnt umber mix into the lower left-hand part of the slope.

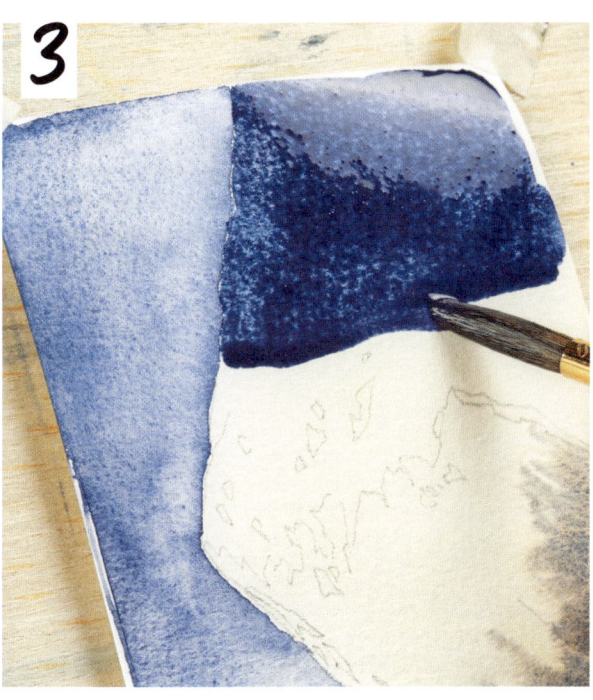

3

▶ Add more French ultramarine to the sky mix to darken it, then turn your paper and block in the shadow area on the right-hand side of the mountain. Draw the paint back and forth evenly to ensure the area is covered smoothly, trying to keep a 'bead' of paint as shown.

Handling complex shapes

Physically turning the painting lets us work from the shortest edge, allowing us to block in the large area quickly and evenly before we reach the small, detailed areas that need to remain as clean white paper. This gives us as much time as possible to work round the details, so there's no need to rush.

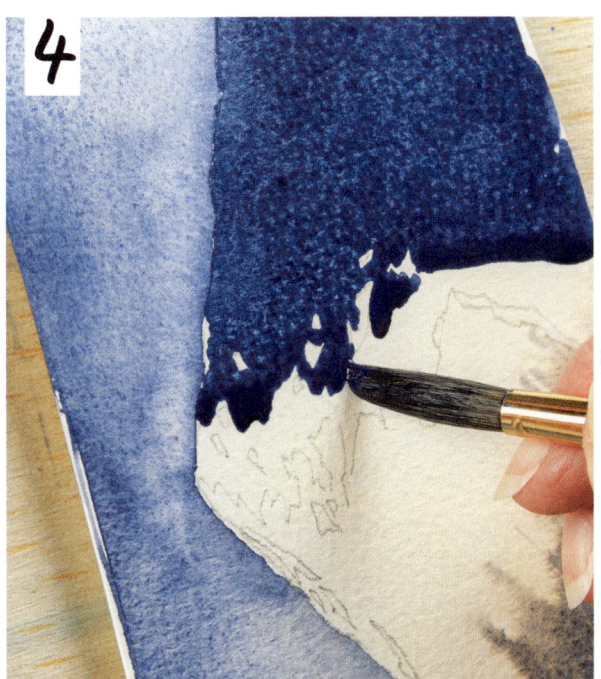

4

▶ Using the point of your brush, draw the bead of paint around the areas of highlight. Continue to paint from side to side, around the shapes, so that the bead remains fluid – this is what will ensure the paint dries evenly for a clean finish.

Keep the paint moving

The main challenge here is painting the pattern of light and shadow on the central area of the mountain. Painting complex shapes can be time-consuming; if you're not careful, you can end up with areas drying at different rates, resulting in backruns and a patchy finish. To avoid this, work from one edge and keep the bead of paint moving.

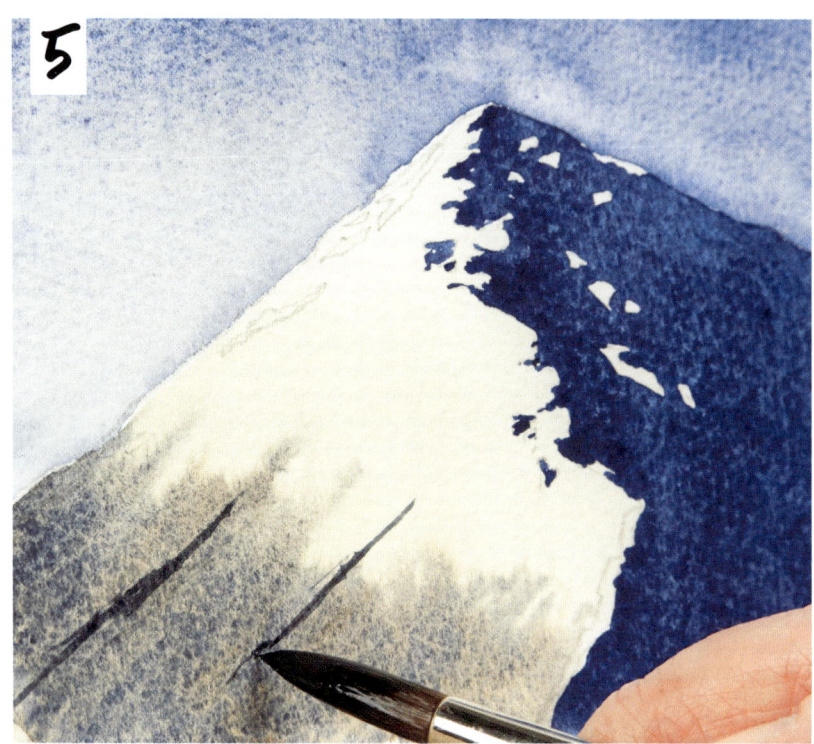

▶ Continue to paint down to the line that marks the end of the shadow area. While you wait for the paint in the main shadow area to dry, use any remaining paint to add the small areas of shadow on the light side of the mountain, then use a strong mix of French ultramarine and burnt umber to indicate the gullies on the slope with diagonal strokes.

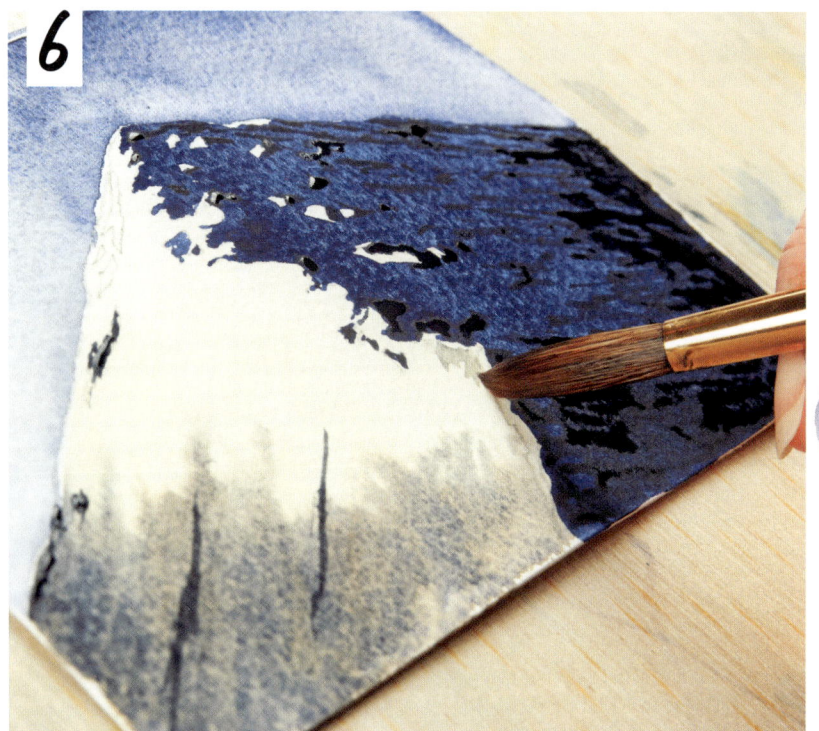

▶ Using a strong mix of French ultramarine and burnt umber paint in the rocks on both the shadow and sunny sides of the mountain. To highlight the sunny side of the mountain, paint the small yellowish rocks on the top left with raw sienna and a tiny amount of French ultramarine.

Keep going

If you accidentally paint over an area that's meant to be left white, don't stop. Carry on, and simply create another nearby.

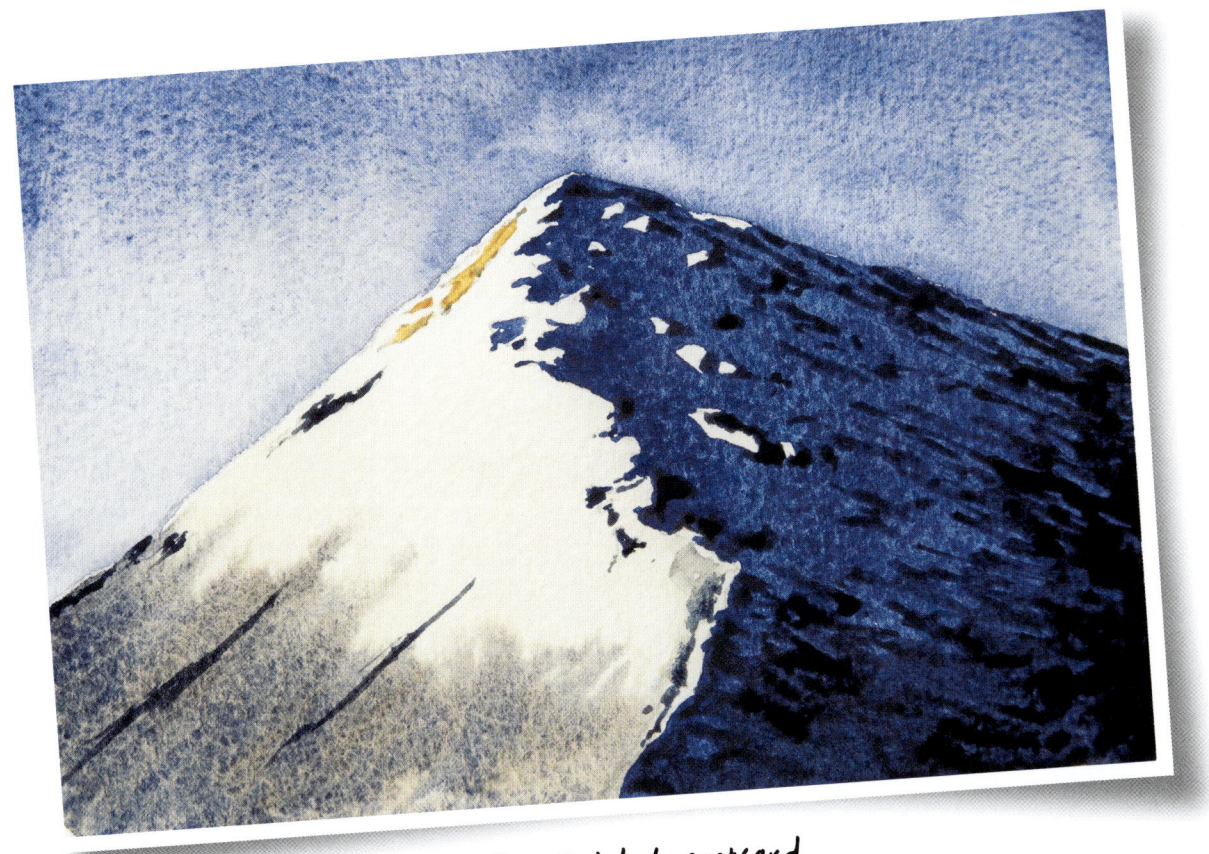

The finished postcard

Ridgeline

A tendency among beginner artists is to give everything an edge even when it's impossible to see one; we feel a compulsion to depict what we know is there. It's often better to trust your eyes and paint what you see, or to change what you see in order to create more interest.

YOU WILL NEED

Paint colours: French ultramarine, cobalt blue, burnt umber, raw sienna

Brush: size 10 round

Other: outline drawing on page 93 (top)

Lost and found edges

An edge you can see is known as a found edge; an edge you can't see is a lost edge.

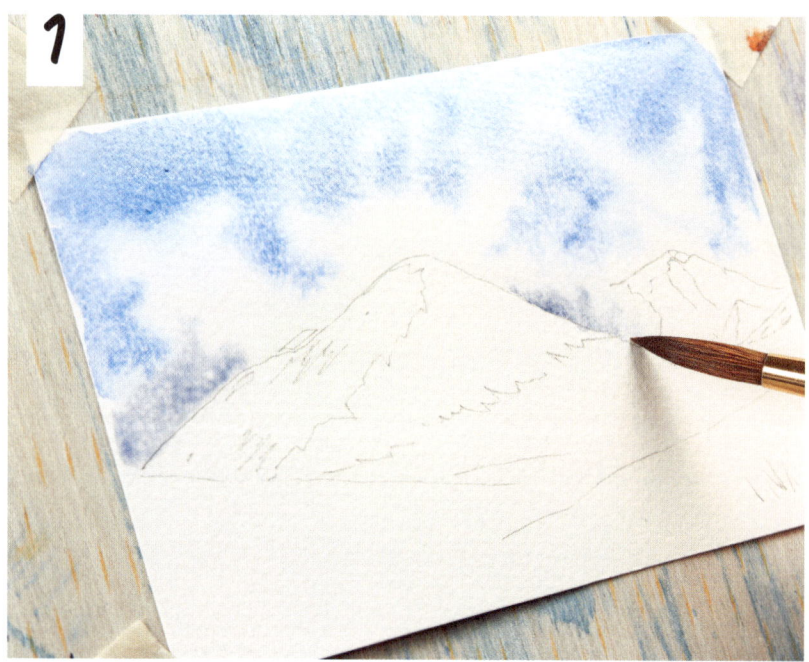

1

▶ Wet the sky, including the valley between the mountains. Drop in cobalt blue to the top, and a French ultramarine and burnt umber mix for the grey clouds; allow this to come into the valley.

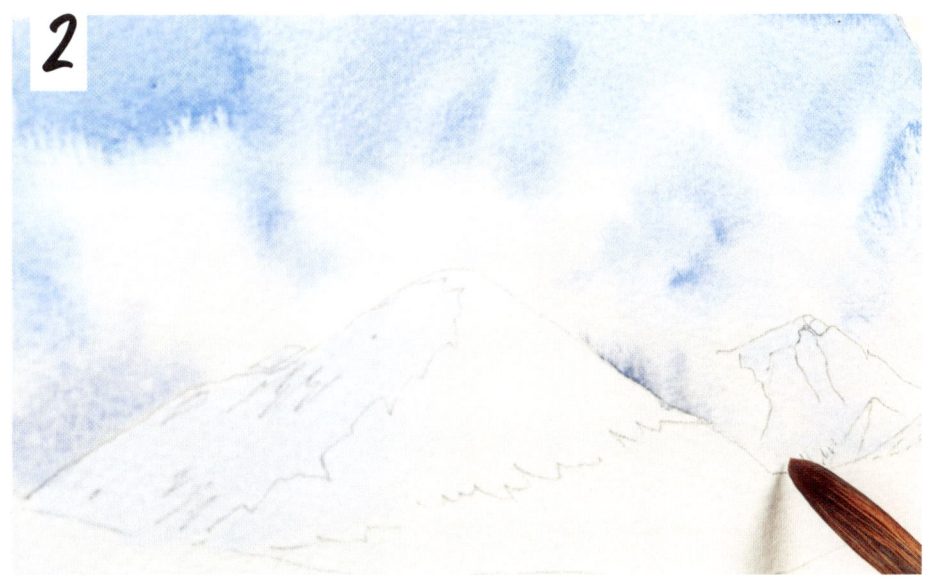

2

▶ Paint the mountains with pale cobalt blue, omitting the right-hand side of the large mountain; soften the edge towards the unpainted side but leave plenty of white.

Counterchange

For dramatic effect in your work it can also be useful to use an effect called counterchange. This is the contrasting of light with dark and dark with light. If it doesn't occur naturally in your subject, you can create it by moving objects around, or by introducing lights and darks as necessary. Here the clouds create subtle counterchange. If the shadow side of the hill had been placed beside a similar tone of sky, instead of a light sky, the effect would be lost.

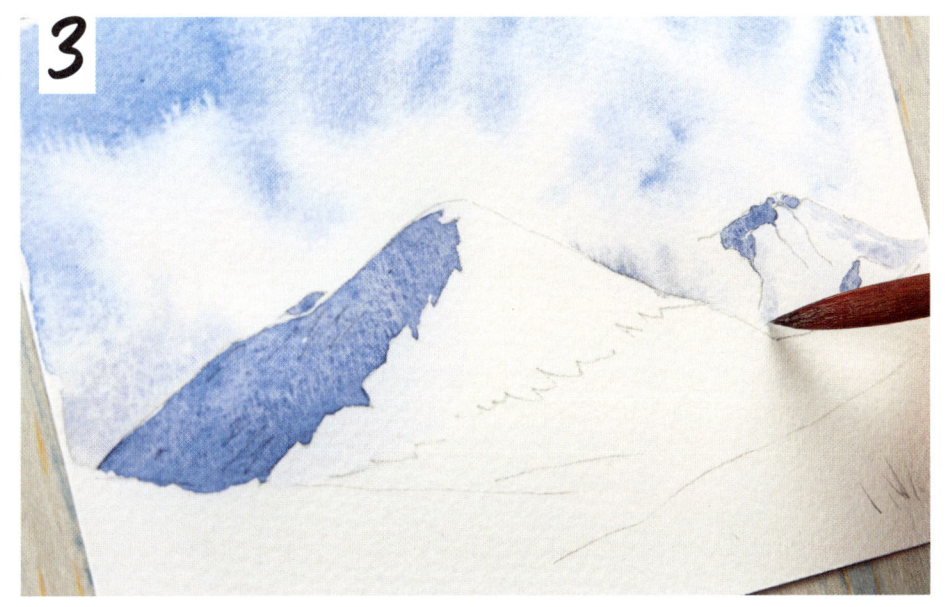

3

▶ Using a midtone mix of French ultramarine and burnt umber, paint the shadow areas of the snow.

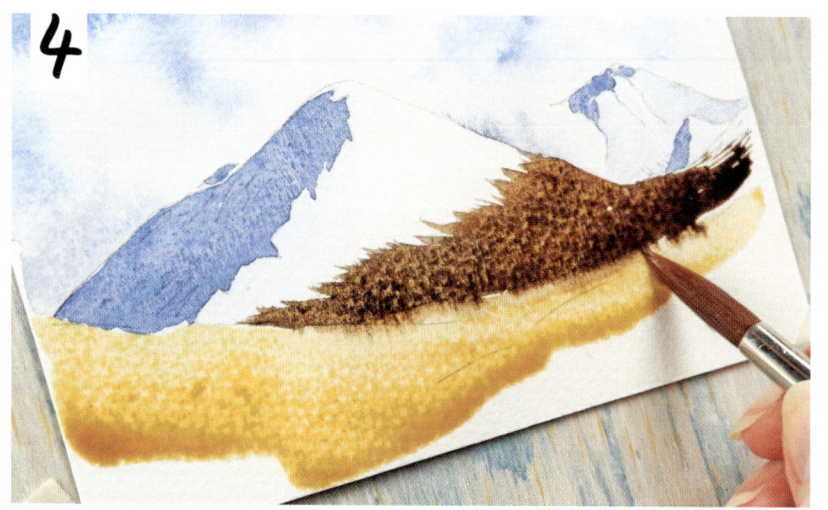

▶ Using a brown mix of French ultramarine and burnt umber, paint the lower slopes of the mountains, changing to raw sienna for the foreground. To create interest here and there, drop in a little French ultramarine and burnt umber to the raw sienna.

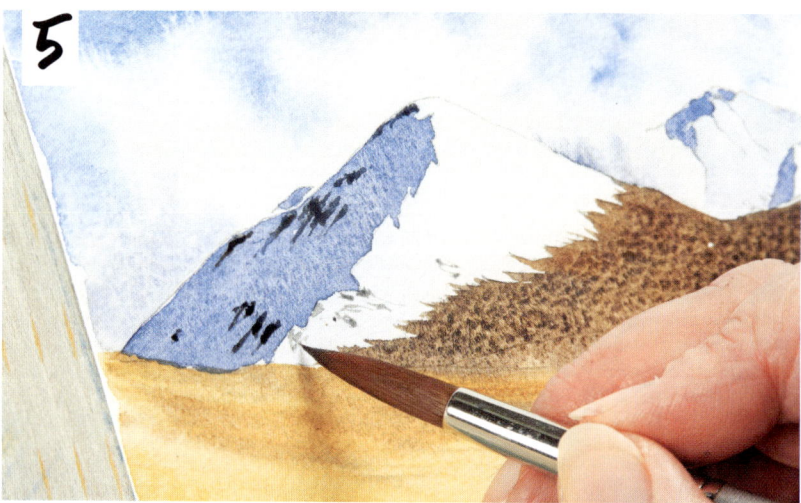

▶ Add darker detail with a mix of French ultramarine and burnt umber for the rocks in the snow on the left-hand mountain.

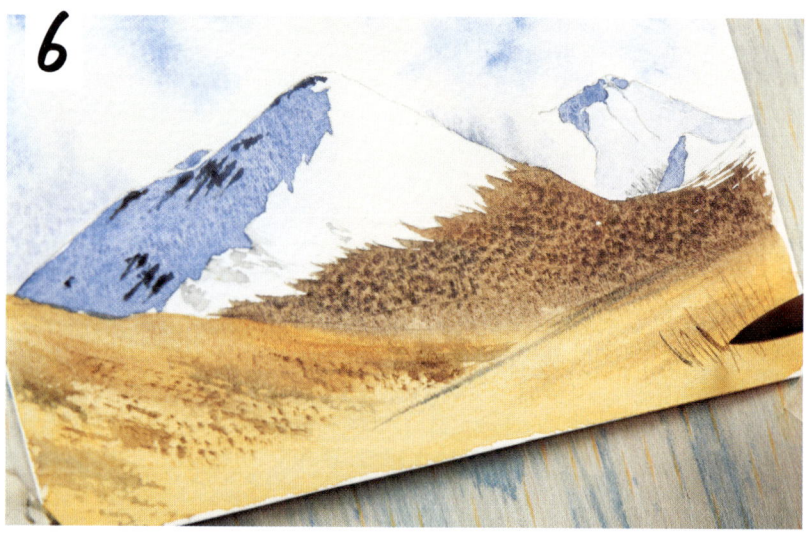

▶ Dry brush the French ultramarine and burnt umber mix onto the foreground on the left. Using positive and negative painting (see page 28), create some grasses on the right.

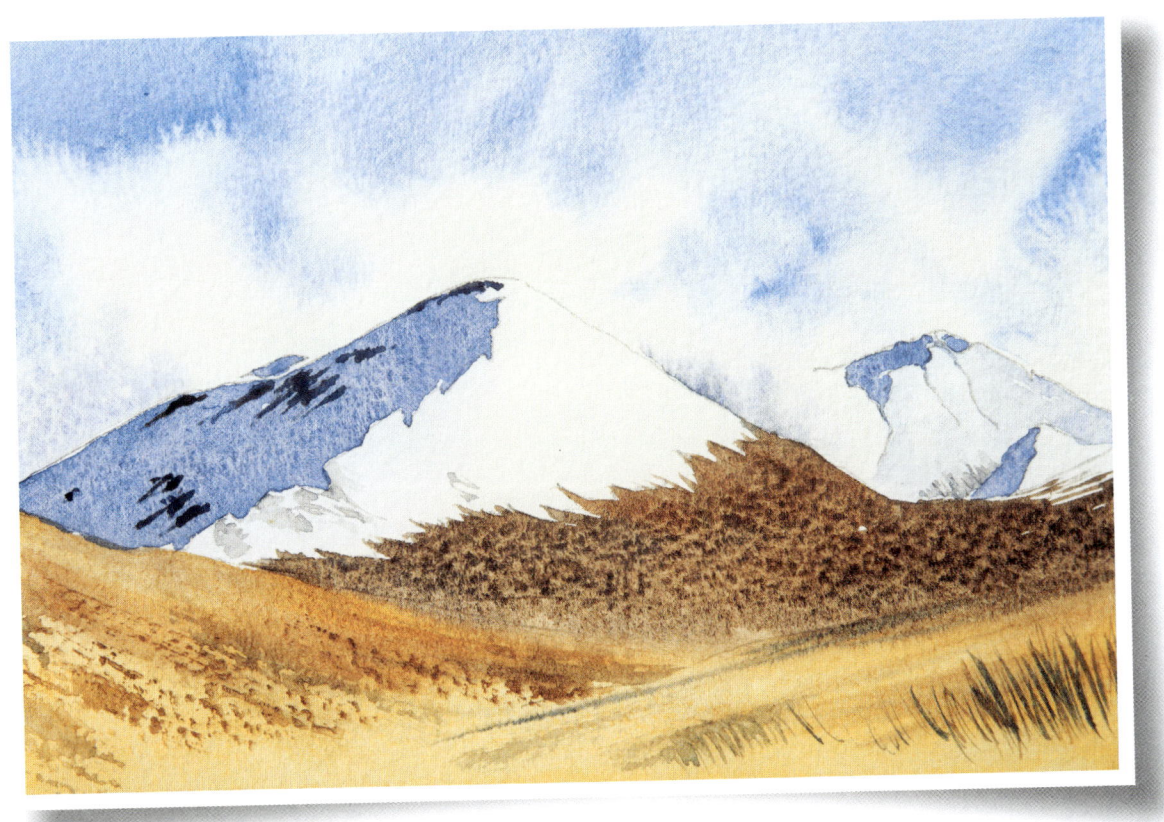

The finished postcard

Silhouettes

Often all we see of a mountain is a silhouette; distance, weather and lighting conditions may make it impossible to see more detail. Mist can reveal much about the contours of a mountain, showing peaks that are not revealed in good weather, and telling us which are closer and which are more distant.

It's very easy to inadvertently create backruns with the softening needed here, so it's particularly important to allow stages to dry completely where noted.

YOU WILL NEED

Paint colours: raw sienna, French ultramarine, burnt umber

Brush: size 10 round

Other: outline drawing on page 93 (bottom), kitchen paper

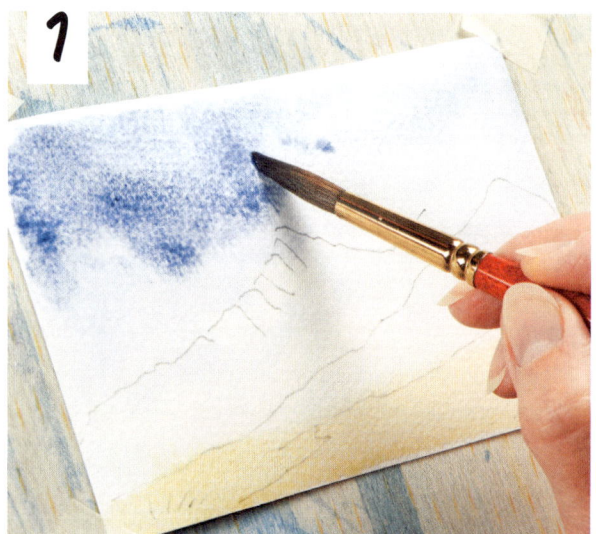

1

▶ Wet the paper all over and drop in a very pale French ultramarine and burnt umber mix to the sky and mountains and raw sienna below, allowing the colours to blend. Drop in stronger French ultramarine and burnt umber at top left.

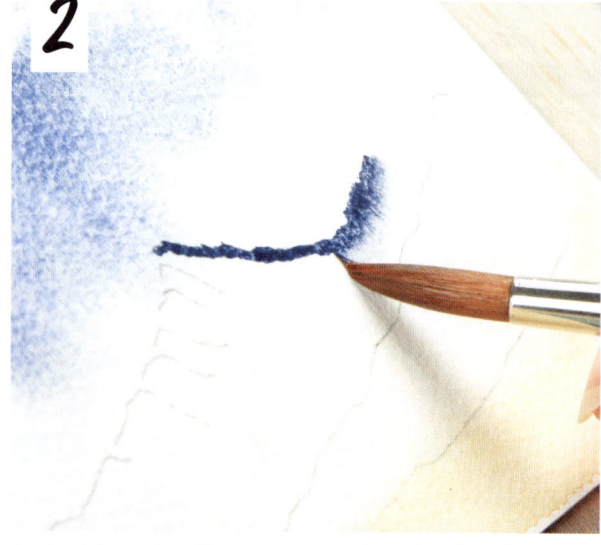

2

▶ Paint the peaks with a stronger mix of the sky colour. If you begin with the tallest pinnacle of the peak on the left and paint alternate pinnacles, you can save on drying time whilst avoiding the risk of one peak bleeding into another. As you paint each pinnacle, soften the underside with a clean damp brush. Allow to dry completely before continuing.

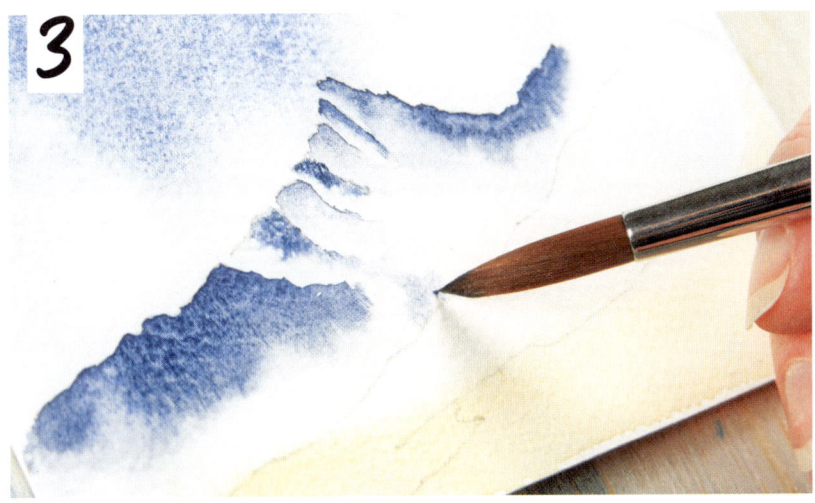

▶ To paint the remaining pinnacles on this peak, paint a stroke of clean water carefully on each. On the area below it, add a little (more concentrated/stronger) colour to each and allow it to bleed.

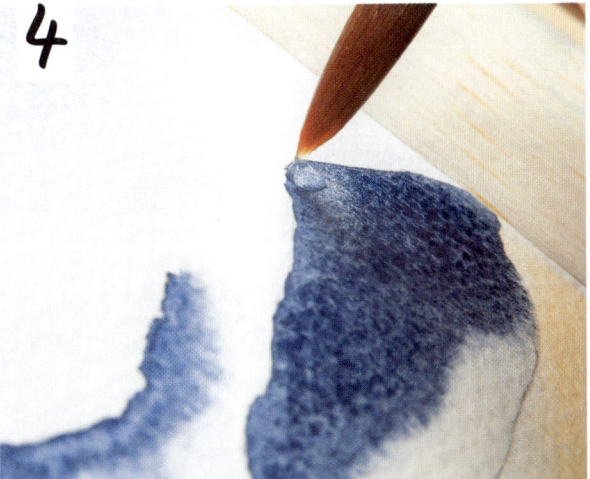

▶ Paint the peak on the right; see if you can deliberately create a backrun at the top by waiting for the peak to dry a little before adding a touch of water.

Creating backruns

Don't be disheartened if you can't create a backrun first time. We usually try to avoid them (see washes on page 12) so deliberately creating one can sometimes be a challenge!

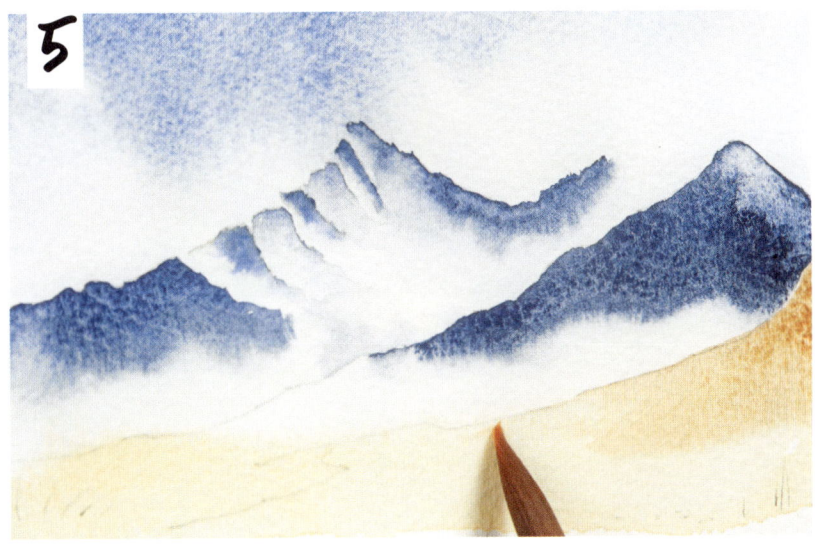

▶ Add burnt umber to the small mountains on the right to suggest proximity; soften the lower edge, then allow to dry completely.

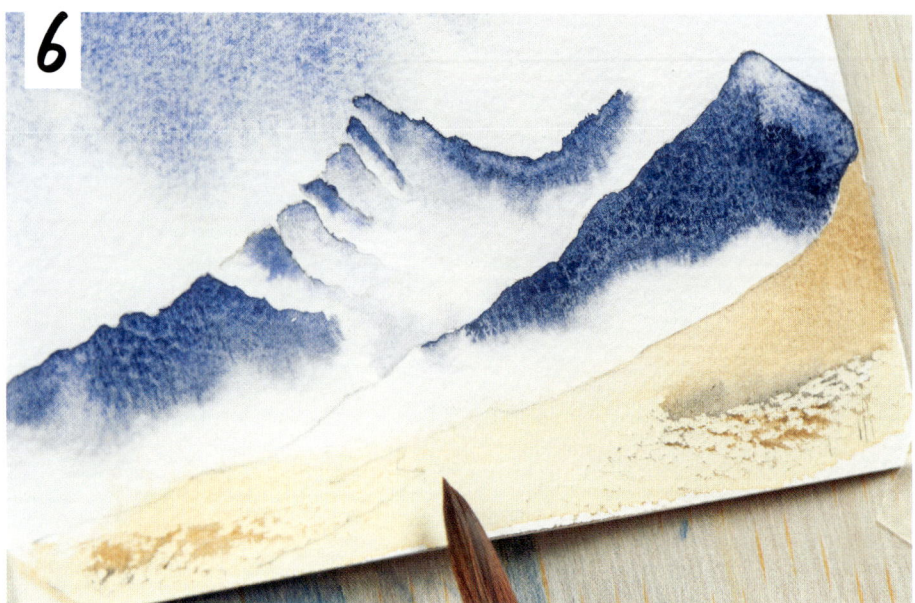

▶ Dry brush a little texture onto the foreground, using French ultramarine and burnt umber. Wash your brush and make another stroke or two in dry brush style, to soften some of the dry brush paint.

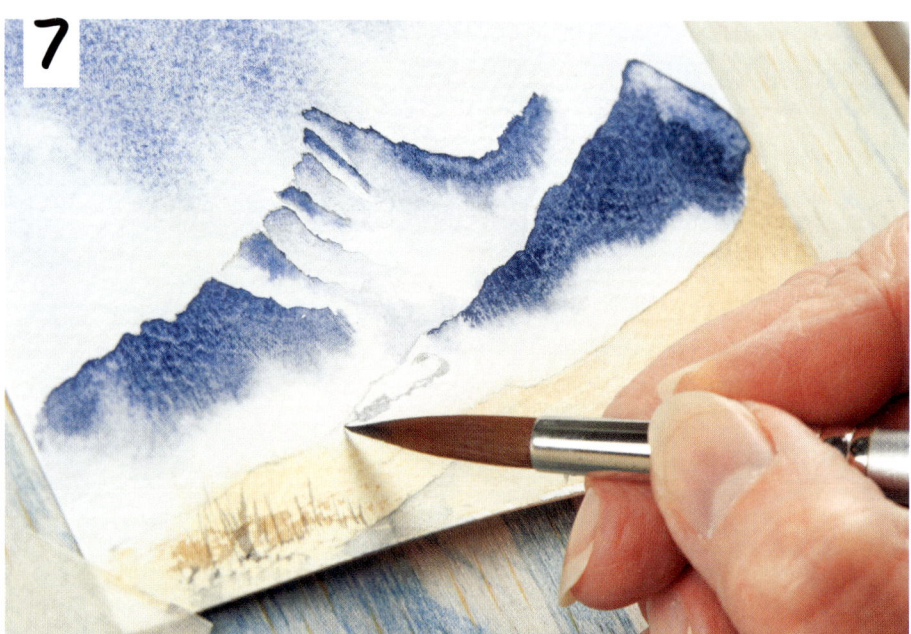

▶ Add more burnt umber to the French ultramarine and burnt umber mix to warm it a little, then use a split brush (see page 22) to add a few foreground grasses, and the tip of the brush for small stones. If any paint has spread too far, lift carefully by gently working with a slightly damp brush and dabbing with kitchen paper.

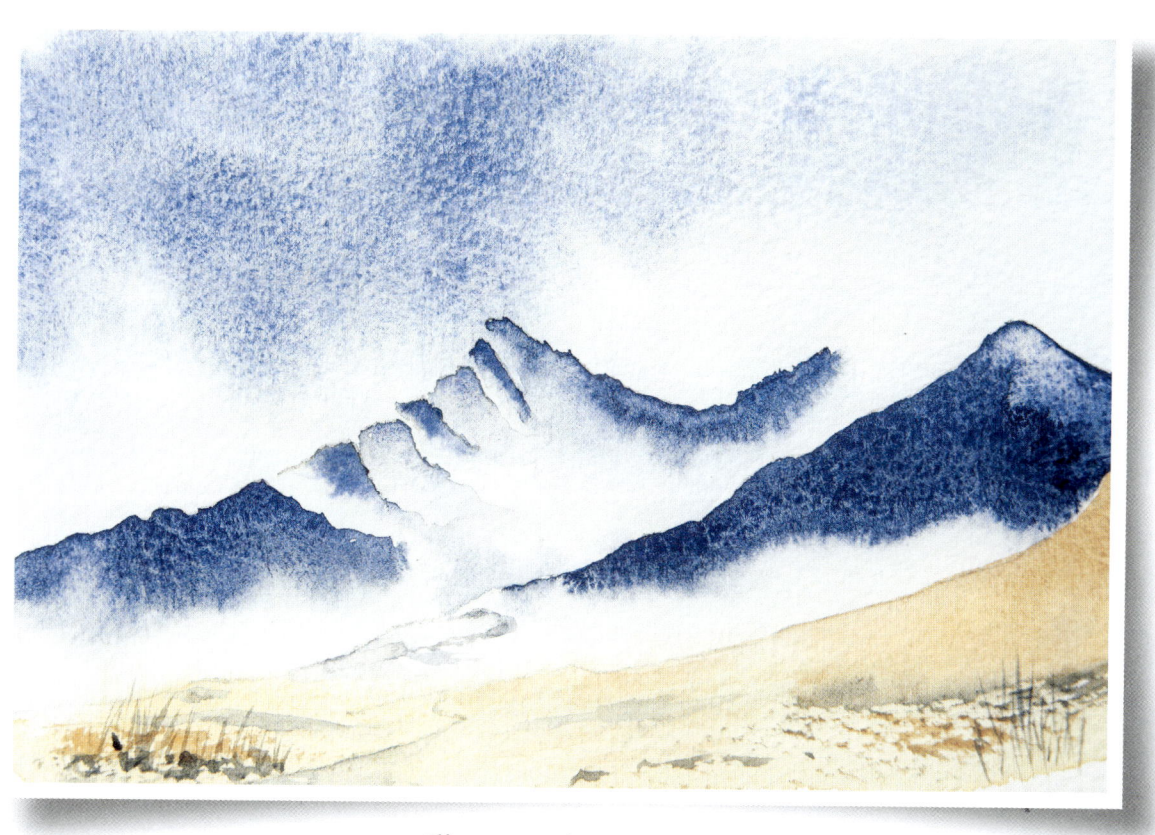

The finished postcard

Bright Water

Light coming from behind or the side of an object creates lovely effects as little 'haloes' of light contrast with shadows; it can turn a dark mass into an interesting arrangement of shapes.

When you come to the foreground in this project, it's important to allow the colour to flow from one rock to the next so that the rocks become a mass instead of individual shapes. Leave the light tops of some rocks unpainted for impact – though if you accidentally paint over one or two it won't matter too much.

YOU WILL NEED

Paint colours: French ultramarine, raw sienna, burnt umber, permanent rose, cobalt blue

Brush: size 10 round

Other: outline drawing on page 94

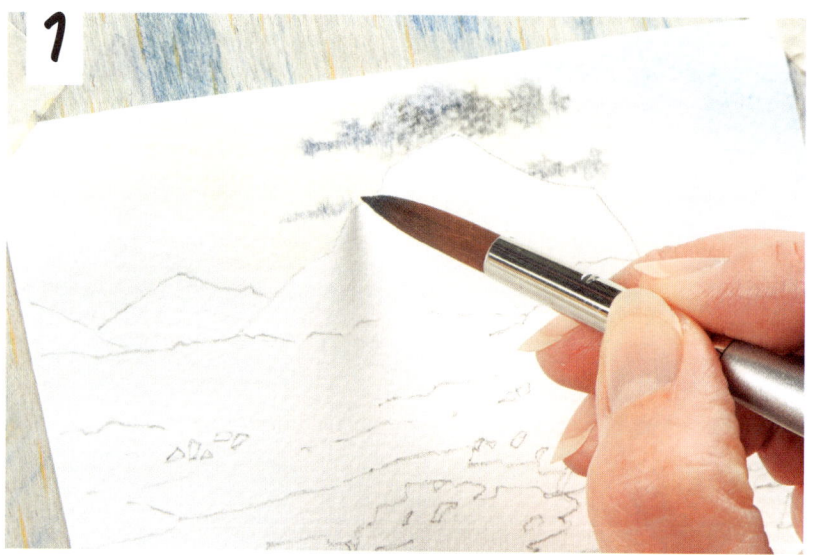

1

▶ Dampen the sky area and drop in very pale raw sienna to the left and very pale cobalt blue to the right. Add a mix of French ultramarine and burnt umber for the clouds, keeping them light and subtle.

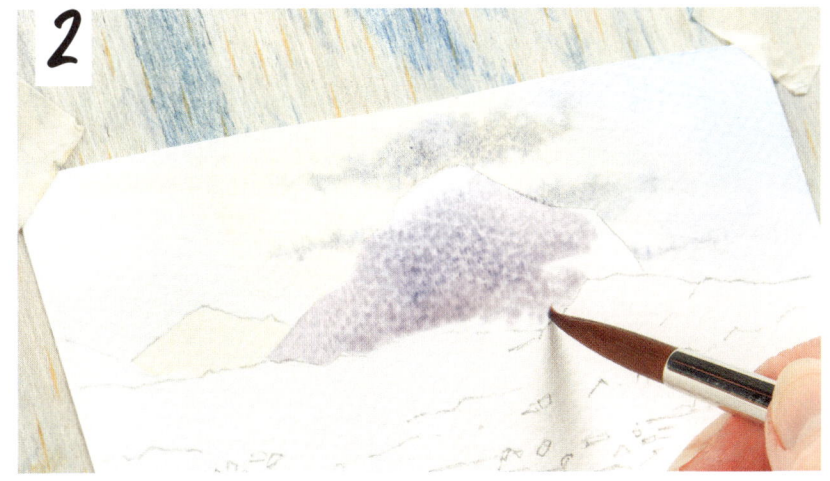

► Using pale raw sienna, paint the most distant hill and allow it to dry. Wet the peak of the larger central hill with a damp brush, then paint the whole hill with the French ultramarine and burnt umber mix, adding a touch of permanent rose. The wet peak will create a highlight as shown.

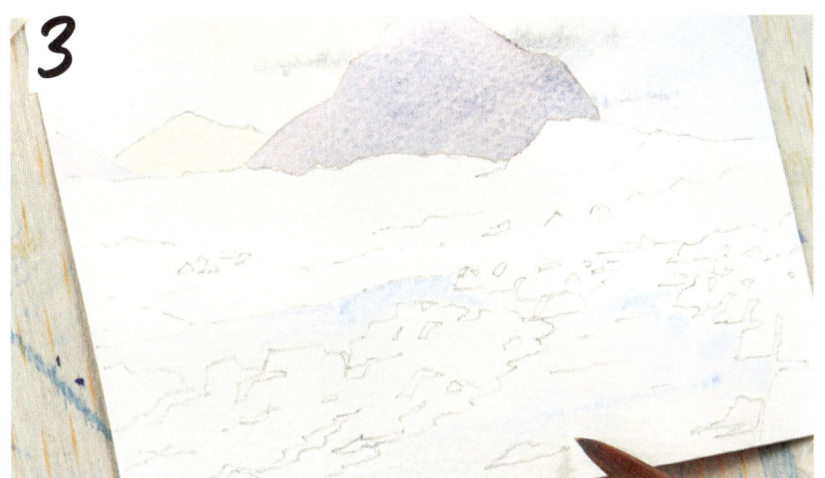

► Paint the smaller hill on the far left of the painting. Next, dampen the water area and drop in pale cobalt blue. This helps to establish the area and make the complex outline easier to 'read'.

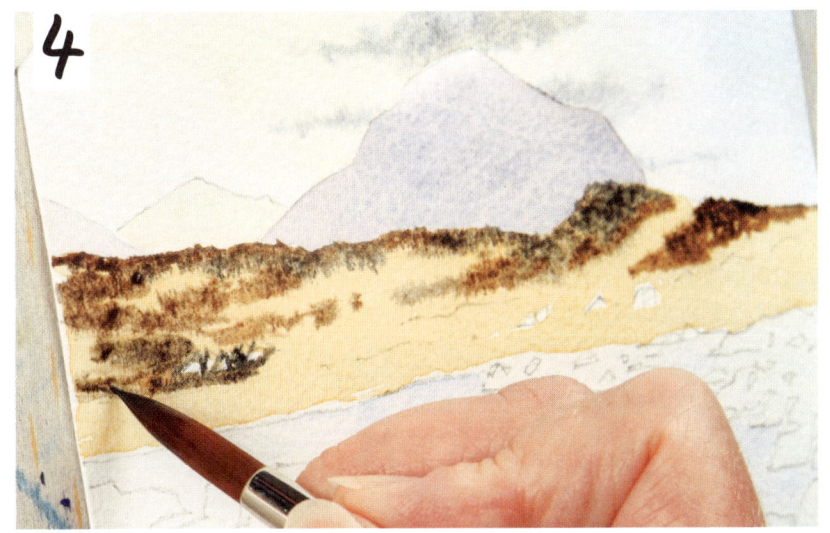

► Cover the moorland with pale raw sienna, then use a French ultramarine and burnt umber mix for both the lower edge of the river bank and to touch in the heather.

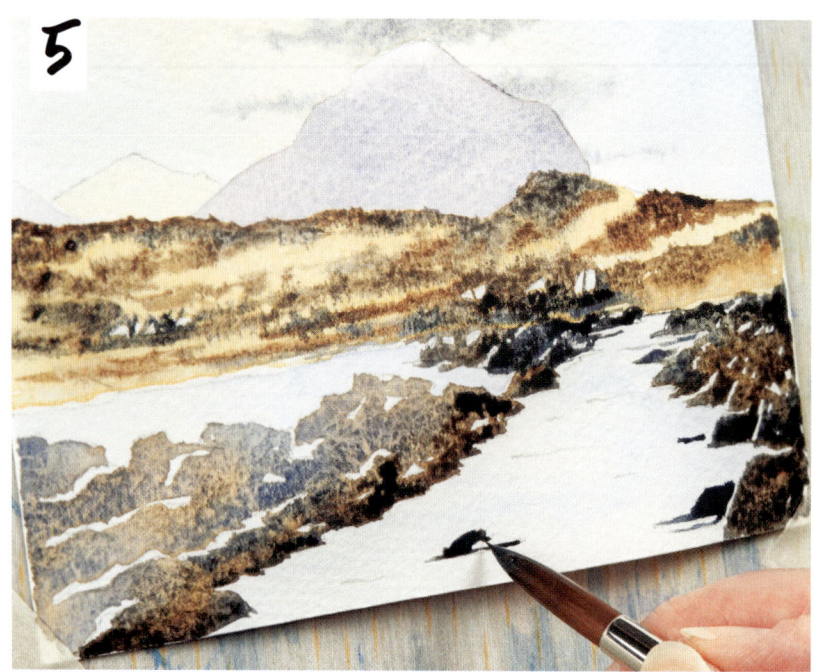

▶ Ensure that you have a reasonable amount of the French ultramarine and burnt umber mix, then begin to paint the rocks. Vary the strength and proportions of colour to give variety, and keep the foreground rocks on the left-hand side generally lighter.

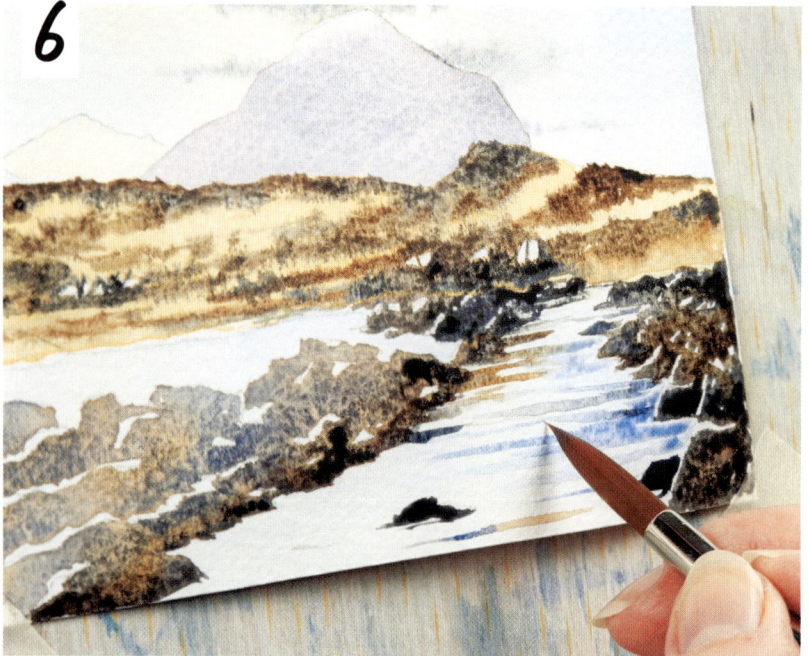

▶ Add medium and darker tones to the water using cobalt blue, French ultramarine and a little burnt umber. Soften the colour in here and there with a damp brush, to suggest reflected colour. Darken the riverbank on the left.

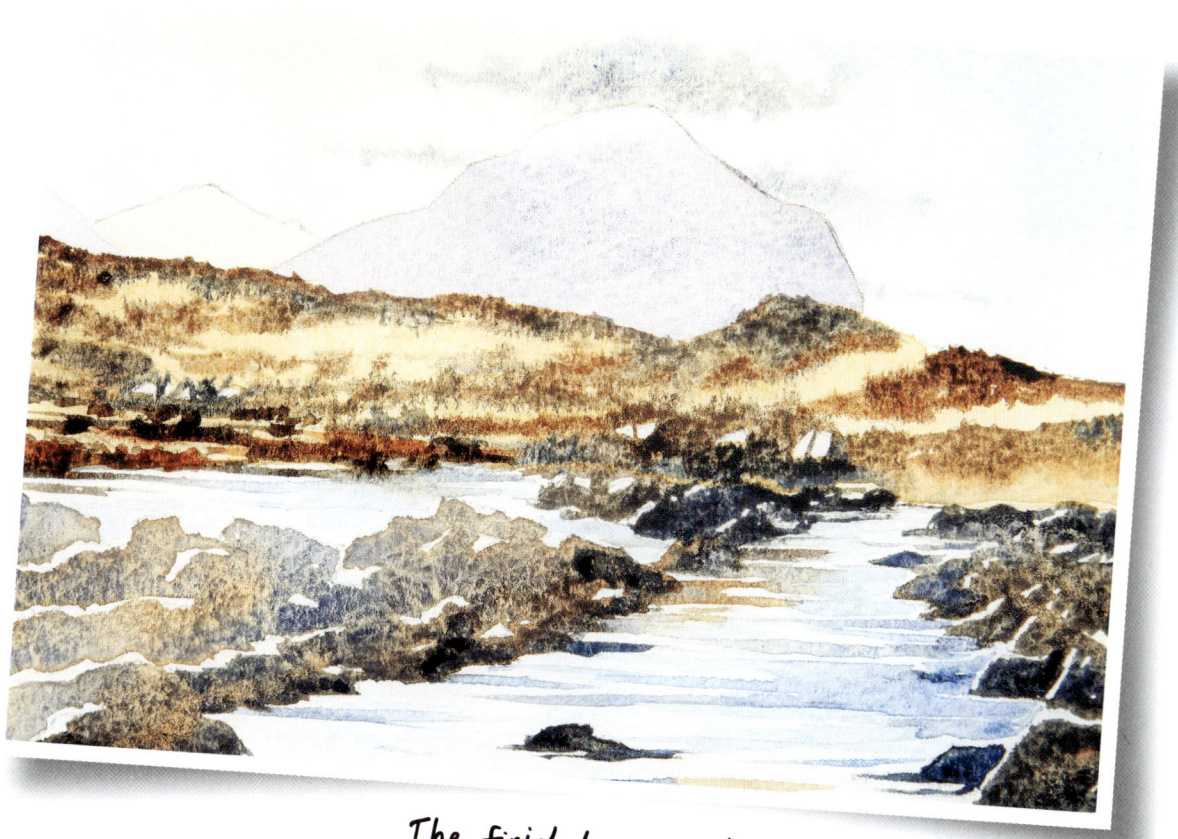

The finished postcard

Wreath of Mist

The beauty of living close to the hills is that you're more likely to catch a magic moment – a mountain wearing a wreath of mist or cloud. Sometimes this effect lasts for hours, sometimes just for moments.

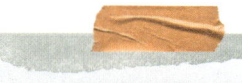

YOU WILL NEED

Paint colours: raw sienna, burnt umber, French ultramarine, cobalt blue

Brush: size 10 round

Other: outline drawing on page 95

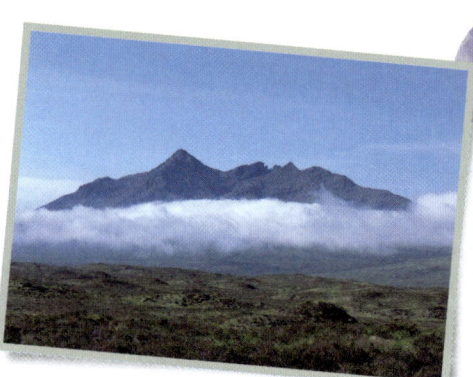

Using photographs

A photograph can be invaluable for capturing subtle effects like the mist shown here. As there might not be time for a sketch, practise your camera skills.

1

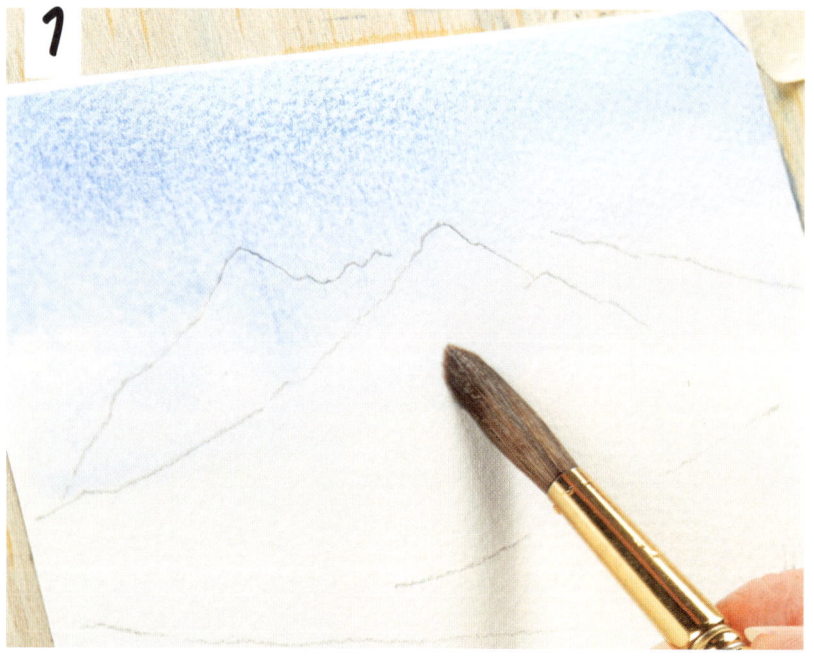

▶ Paint a graduated cobalt blue wash to the sky, bringing the palest tones down over the tops of the mountains.

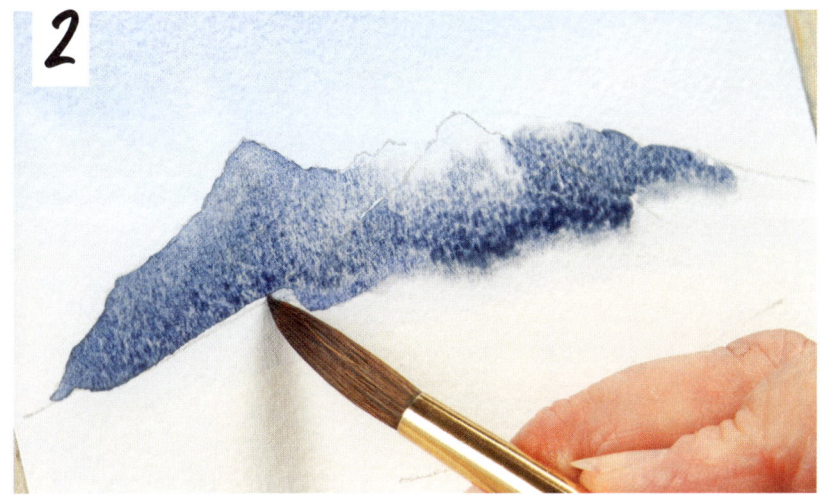

▶ Apply water to the peaks that are to stay white, then paint the mountains with a French ultramarine and burnt umber mix, softening the edges below as shown.

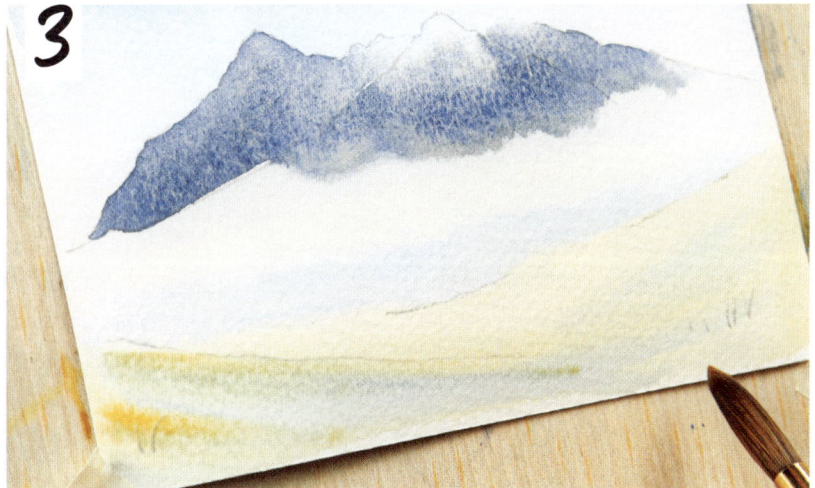

▶ Using very pale cobalt blue, create the lower edge of the mist band, and soften the upper edge of this. Paint the land below with a pale wash of raw sienna, adding a few strokes of pale cobalt blue while this is still damp.

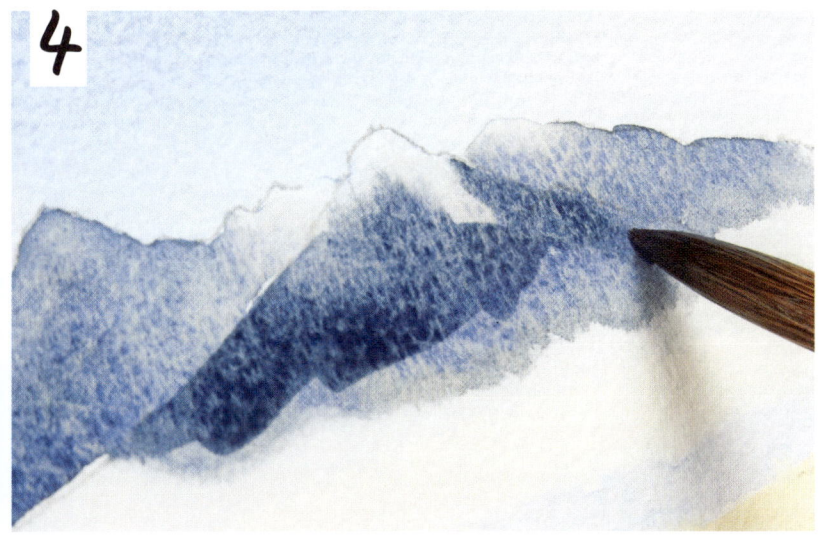

▶ Paint the middle peak again, softening as before.

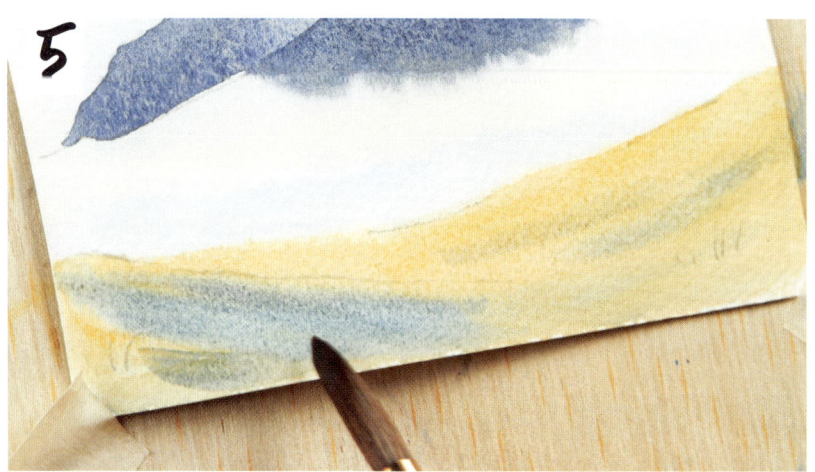

▶ Wash the foreground with raw sienna, then add a few touches of cobalt blue.

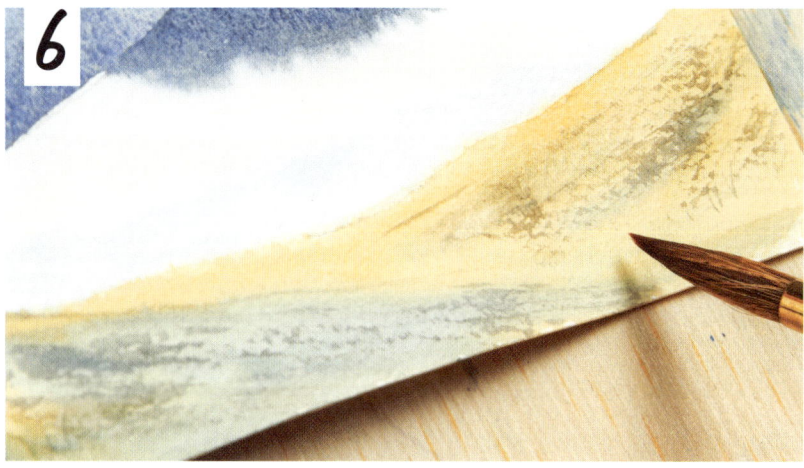

▶ Using a little burnt umber, dry brush texture over the moorland, then dry brush a little clean water through some of this to soften some areas.

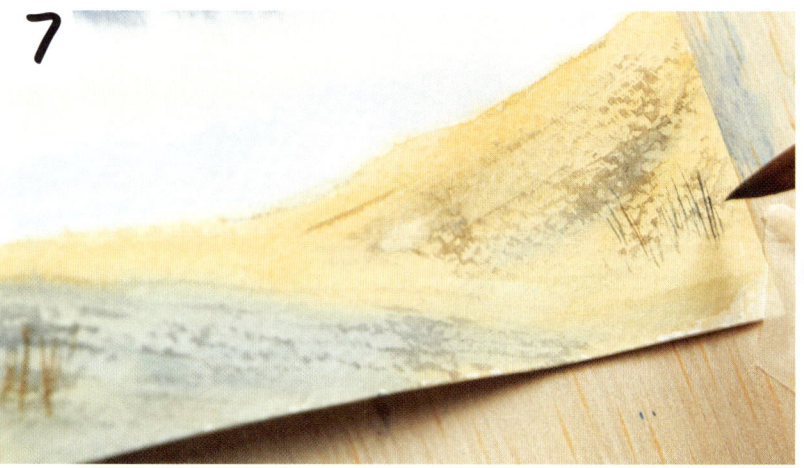

▶ With a little French ultramarine and burnt umber mix on your brush, create a few grasses to give scale to the foreground.

Stray colour

If any colour has strayed beyond where you wished it to go, lift out a little using a damp brush and kitchen paper.

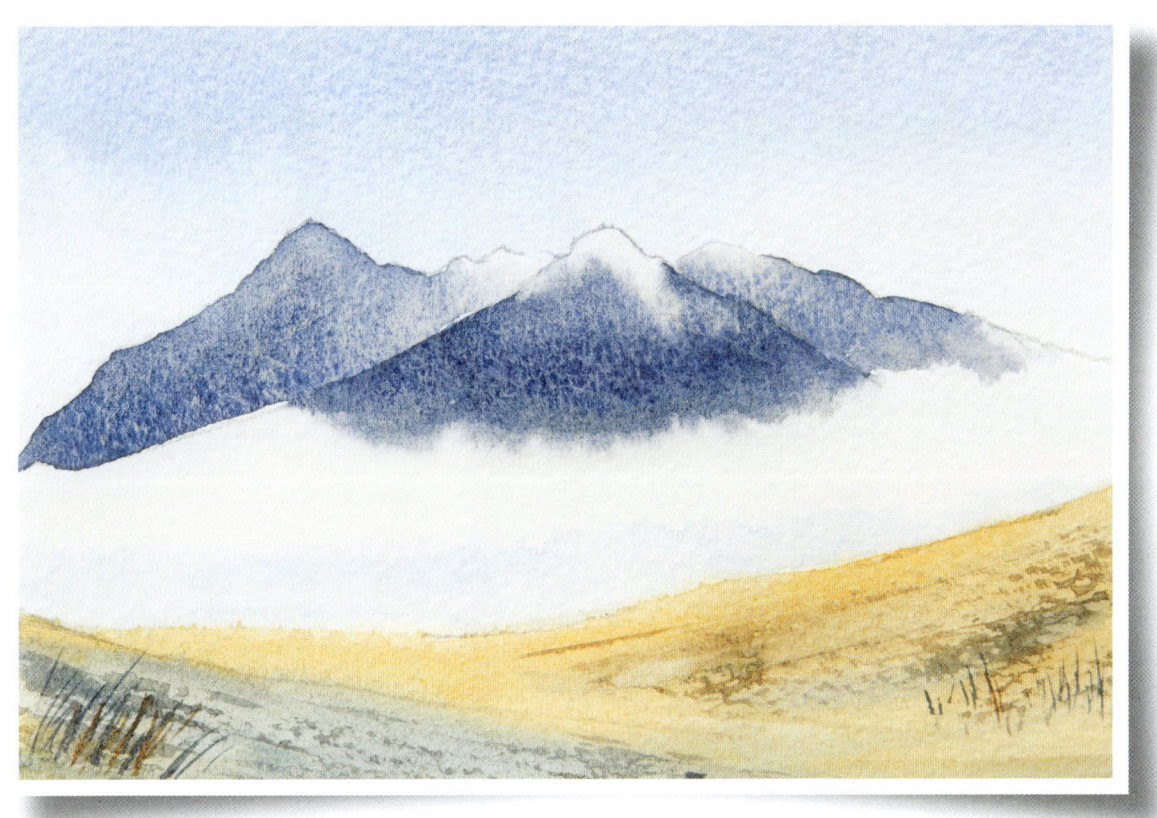

The finished postcard

Outline drawings

An outline drawing is provided for every postcard painting project in this book. If you don't feel confident enough to draw freehand, you can transfer the outline to your watercolour paper by following the simple steps below.

USING TRACEDOWN PAPER

This is an easily available paper for transferring images, sometimes known as graphite paper, and is similar to the carbon paper that was used in the days of typewriters.

1 Slip your sheet of watercolour paper directly under the outline you want to use.

2 Slip a sheet of tracedown paper between the outline and the watercolour paper. Go over the lines using a burnisher or ballpoint pen.

3 Remove the tracedown paper and lift up the outline to reveal the image transferred onto your watercolour paper, ready for you to begin painting.

USING PENCIL

You can transfer the outlines onto your watercolour paper using a pencil and a burnisher or ballpoint pen. If you prefer not to work directly from this book, you can photocopy or scan the outline first, and transfer the outline from a copy in much the same way.

1 Scribble over the back of the outline with a soft pencil.

2 Turn the page so that you are looking at the image you want to transfer. Place your watercolour paper underneath the page. Go over the lines with a burnisher.

3 Lift the page to reveal the image transferred onto your watercolour paper. When you remove the watercolour paper, make sure you put a piece of scrap paper in between this outline and the next to avoid graphite from the back of the drawing transferring onto the facing page.

SEND ANOTHER POSTCARD!

Copies of the outline drawings are available to download free from the Bookmarked Hub. Search for this book by title or ISBN: the files can be found under 'Book Extras'.

Membership of the Bookmarked online community is free: www.bookmarkedhub.com

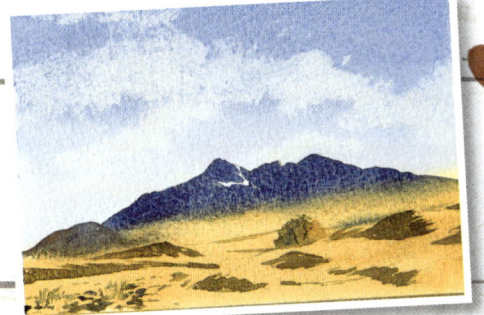

Summer Sky 24

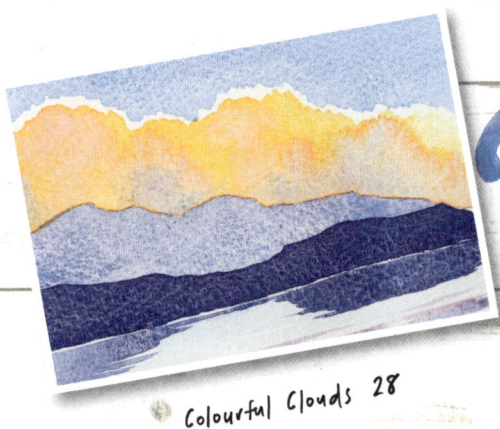

Colourful Clouds 28

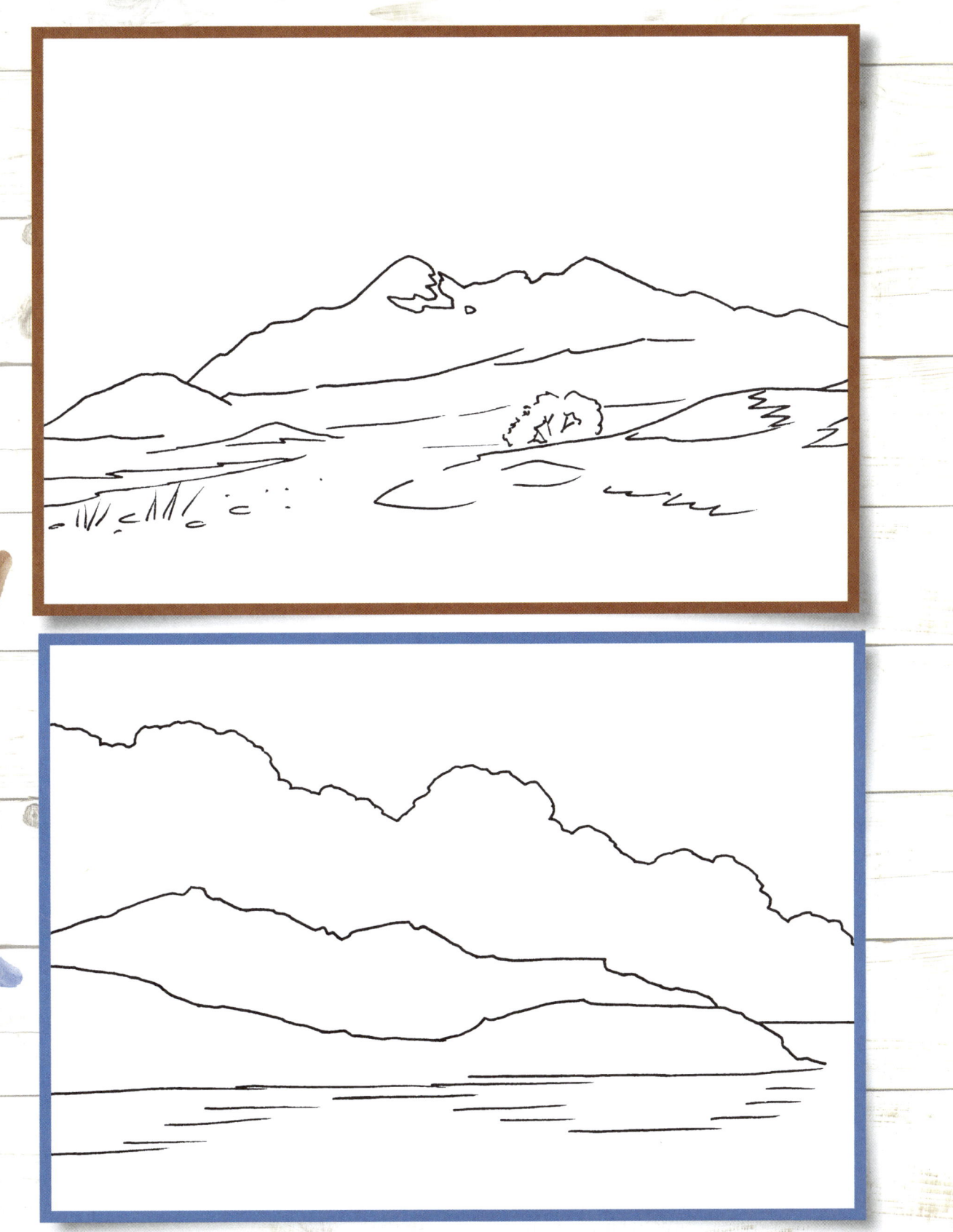

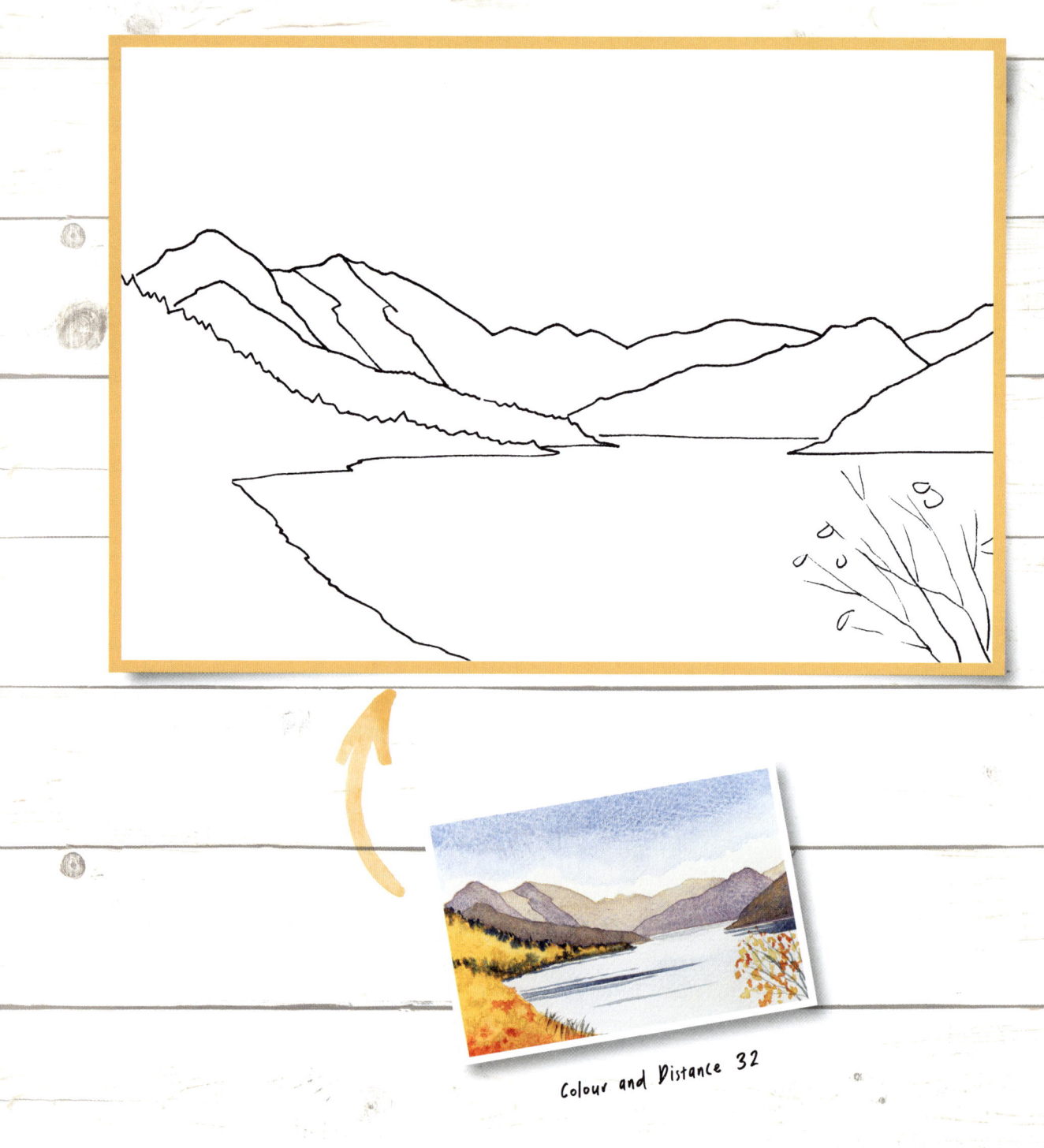

Colour and Distance 32

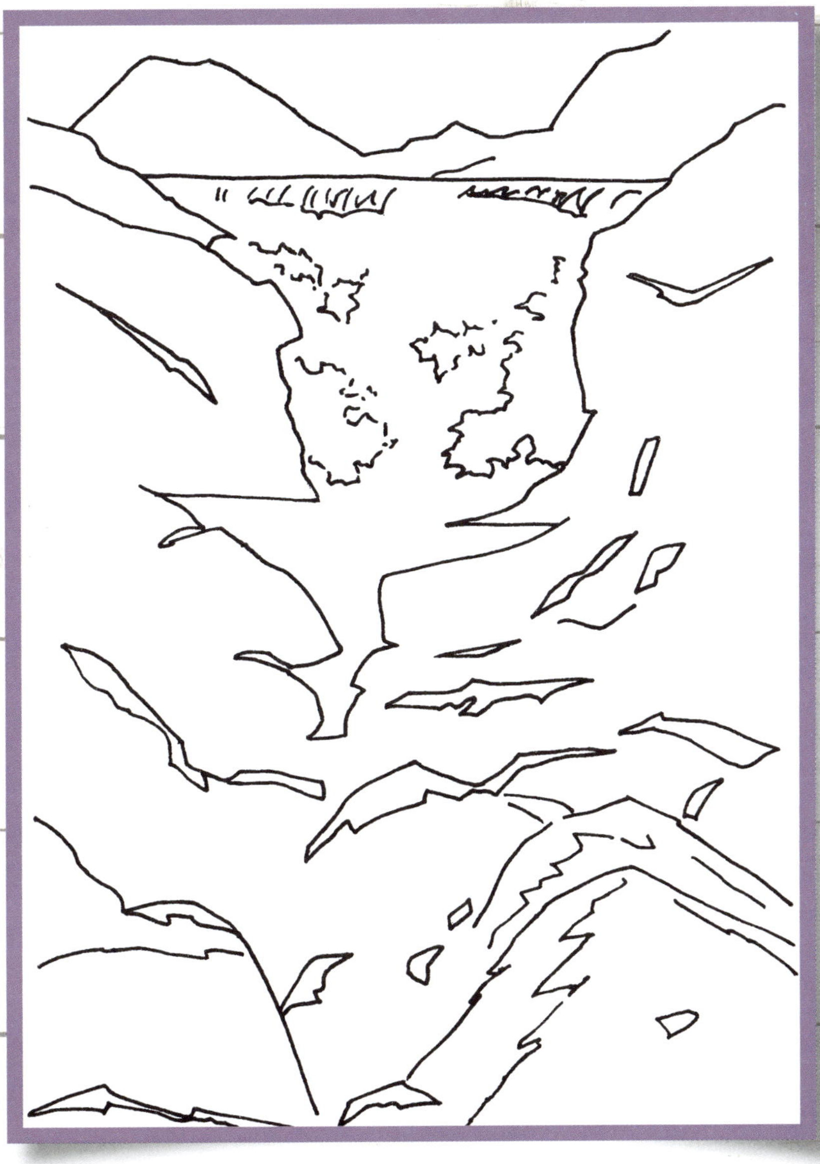

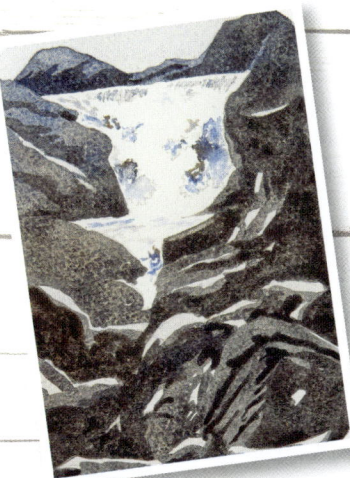

Waterfall 36

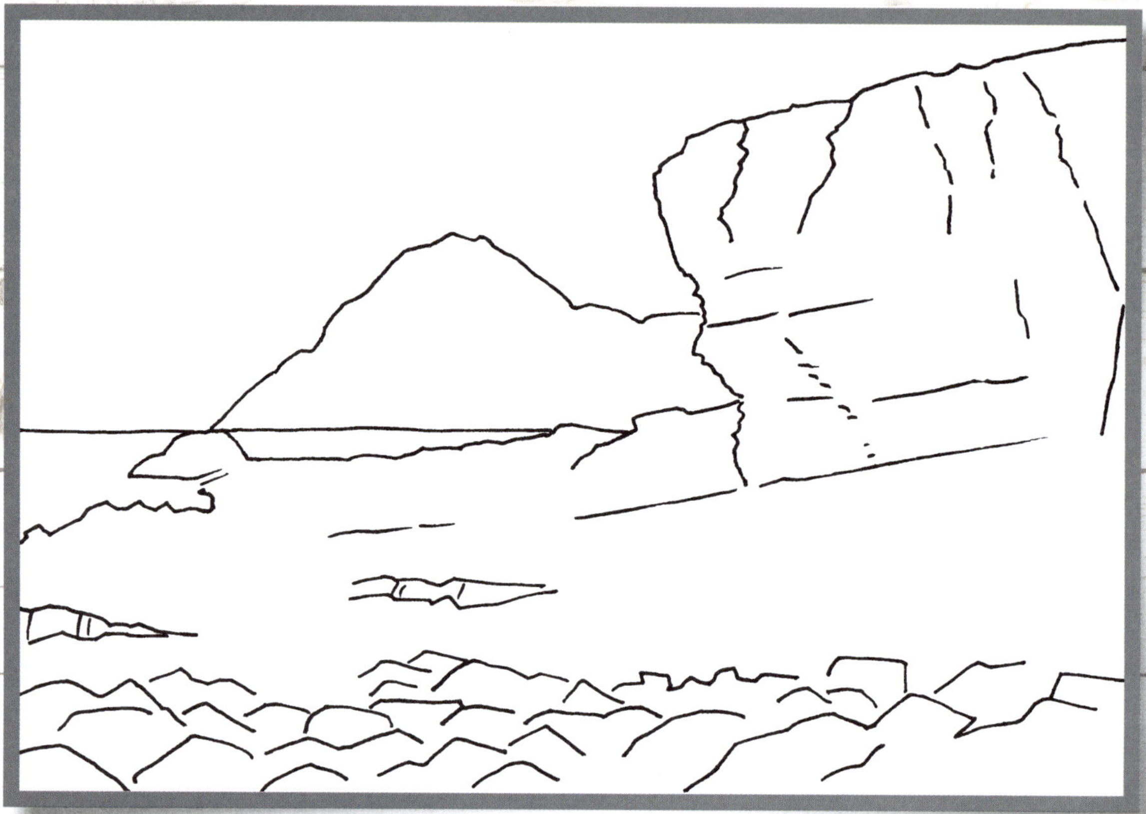

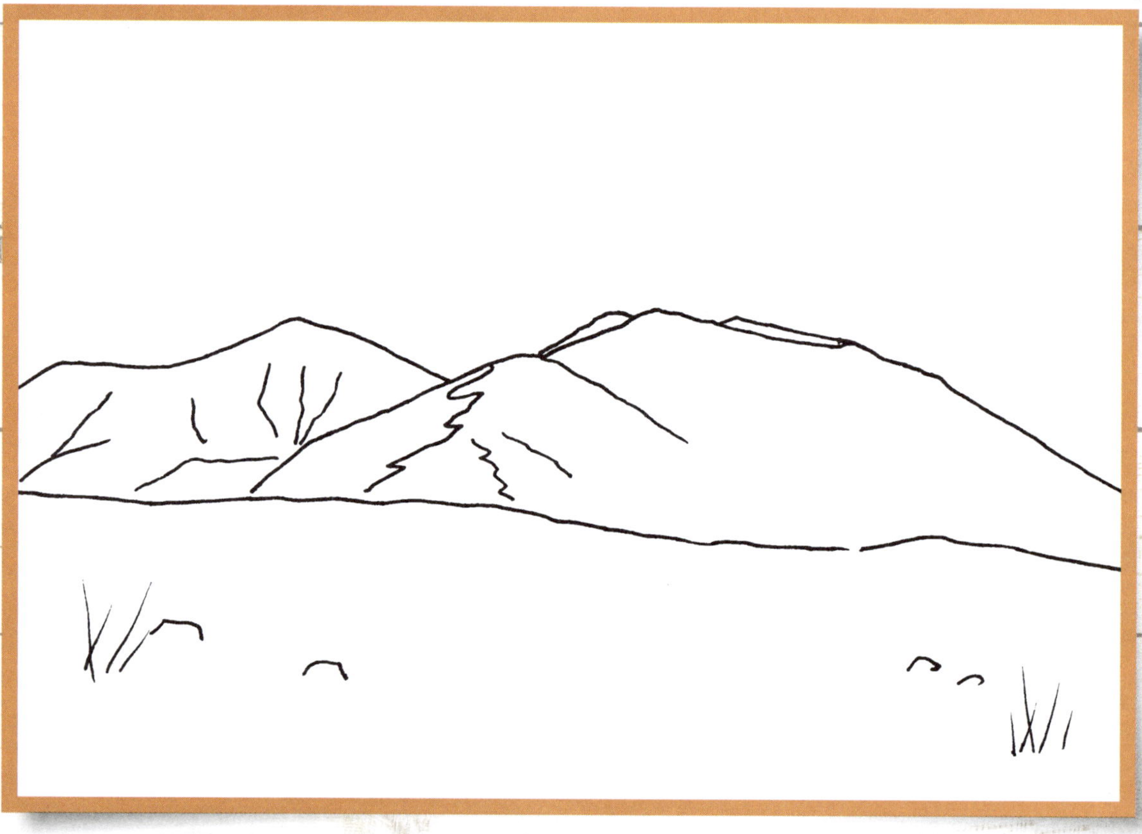

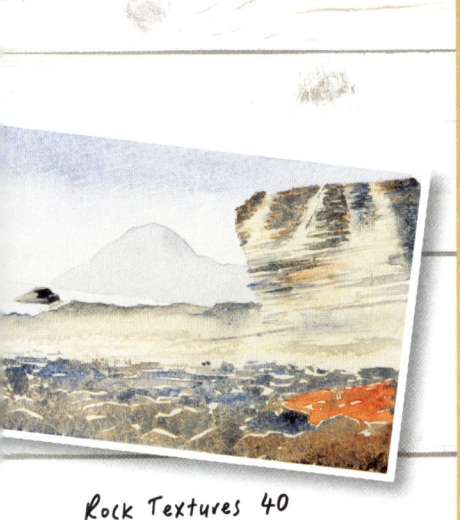
Rock Textures 40

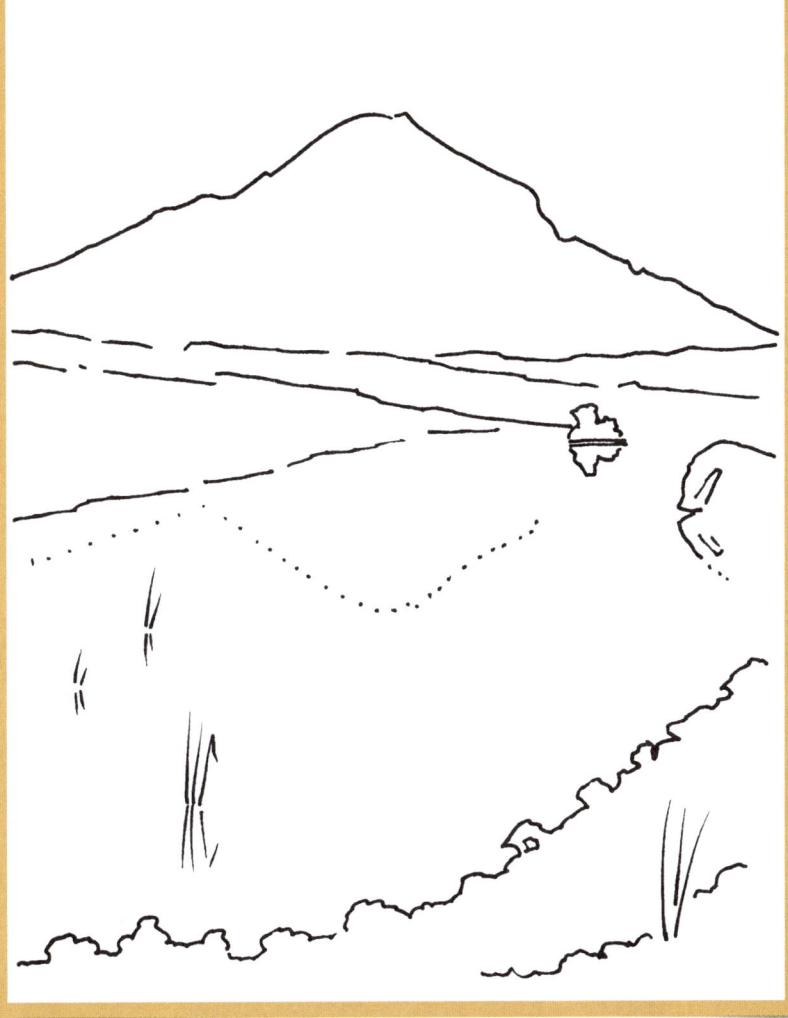

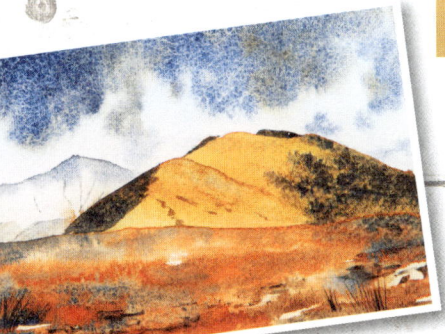
Sunlight and Shadows 44

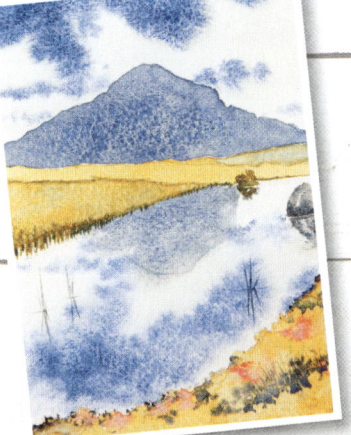
Reflections 48

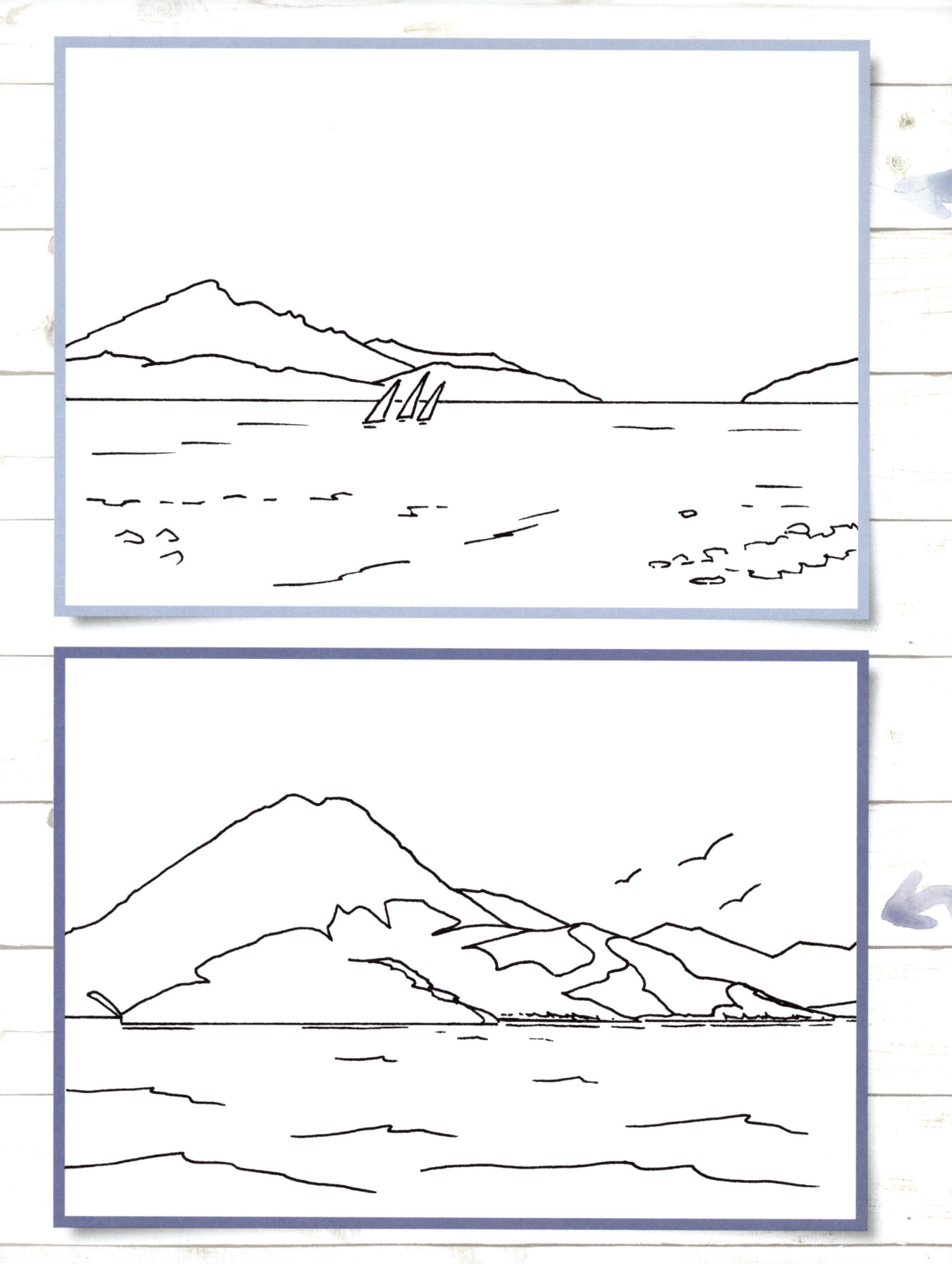

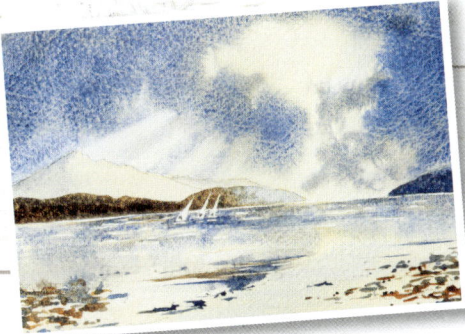

Mountain and Sea 52

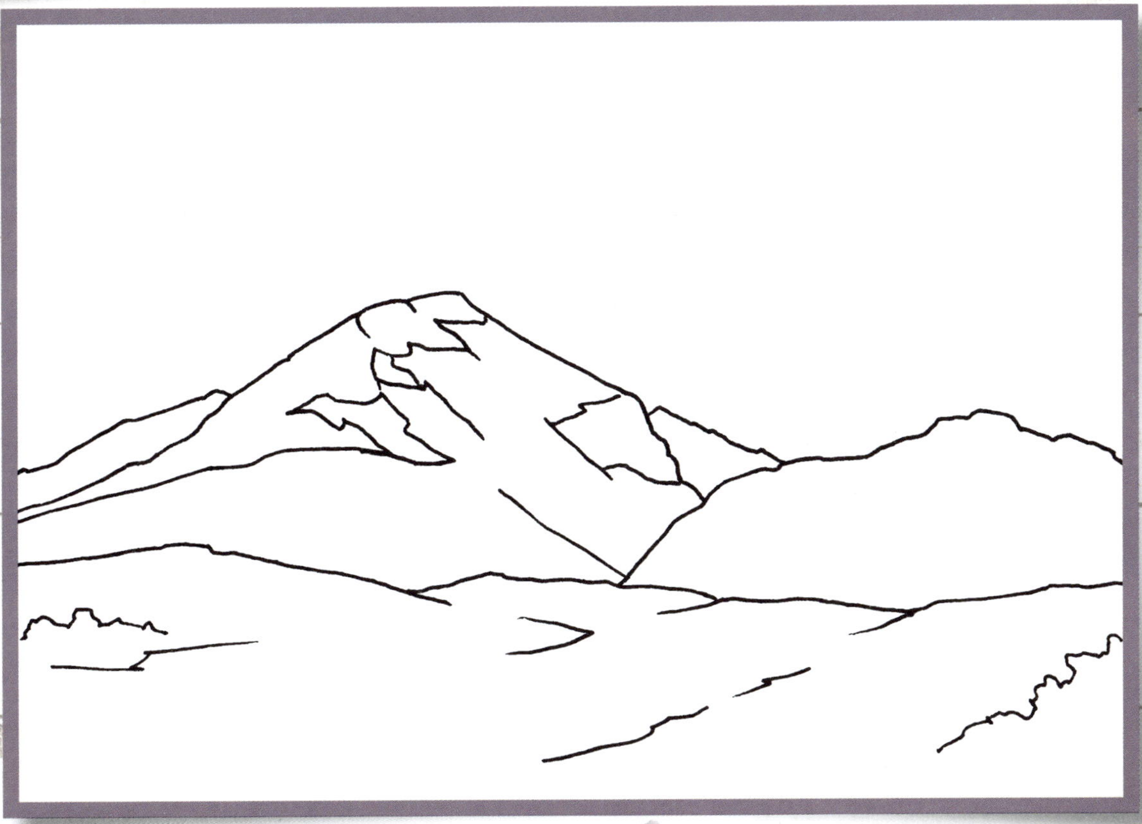

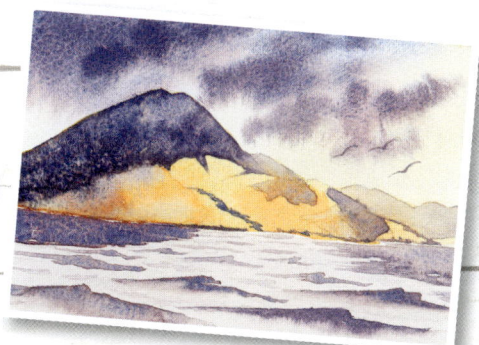

Wavelets and Ripples 56

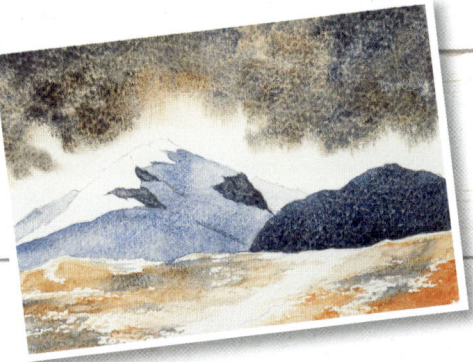

Chill Peaks 60

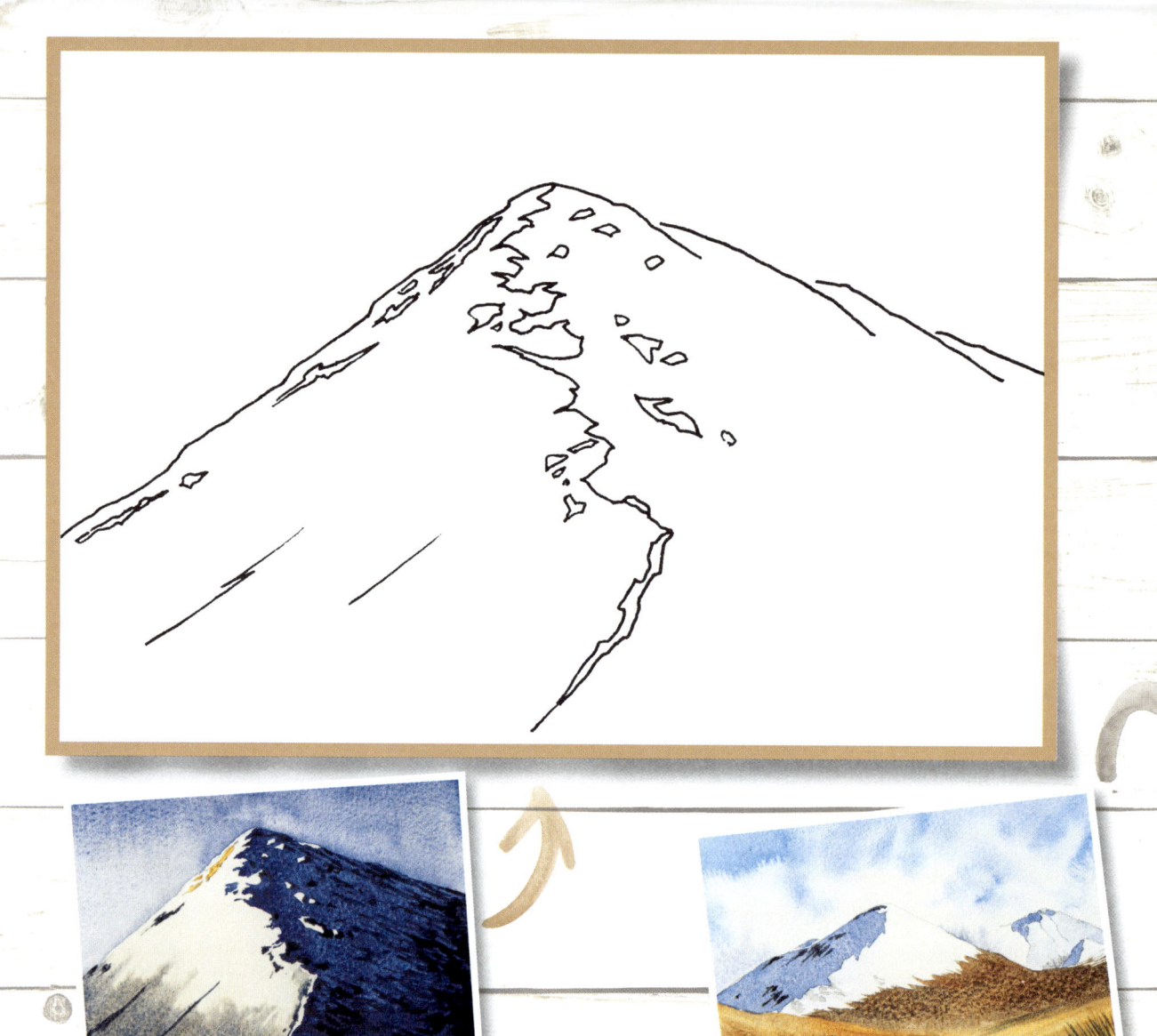

Snowy Summit 64

Ridgeline 68

Silhouettes 72

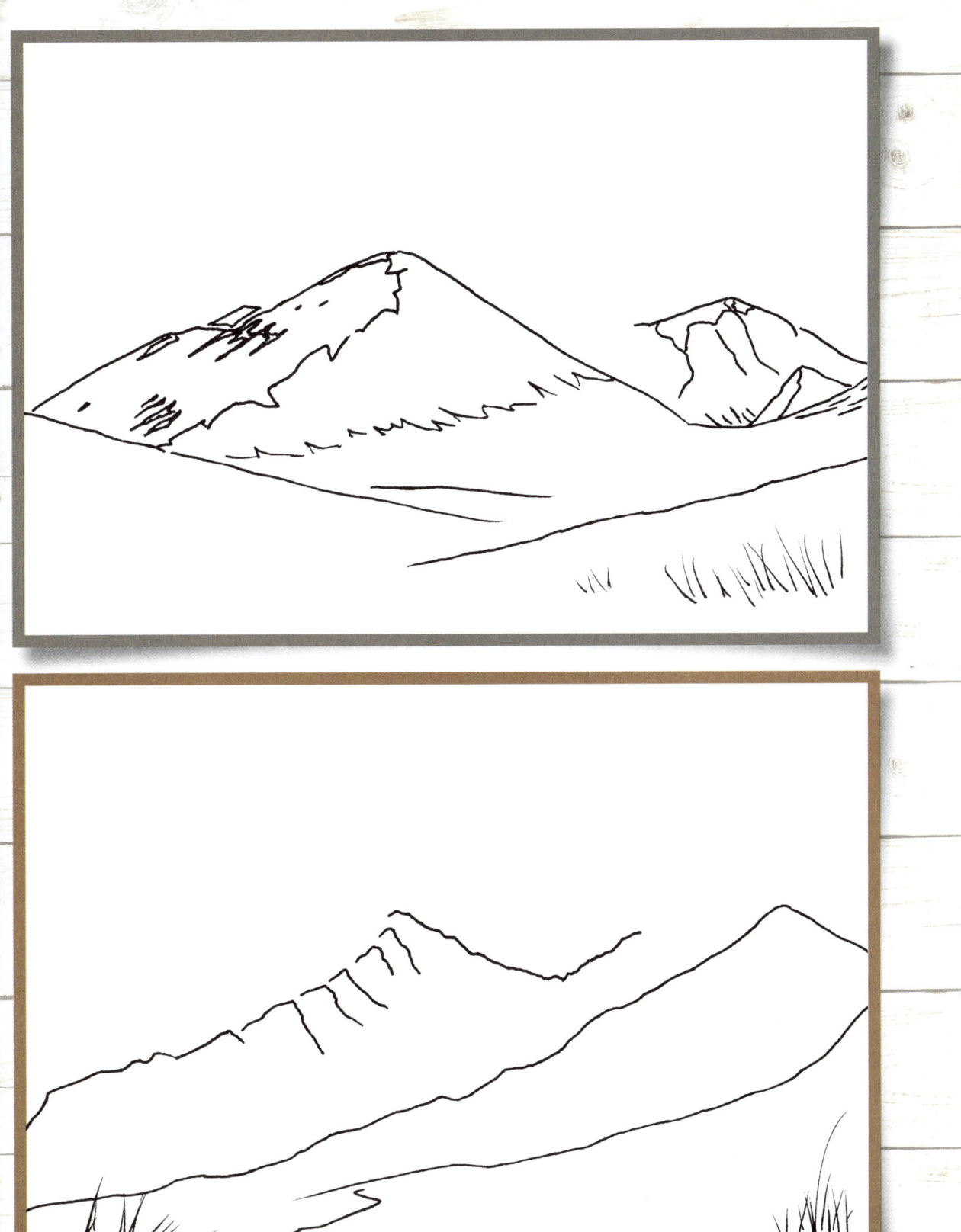

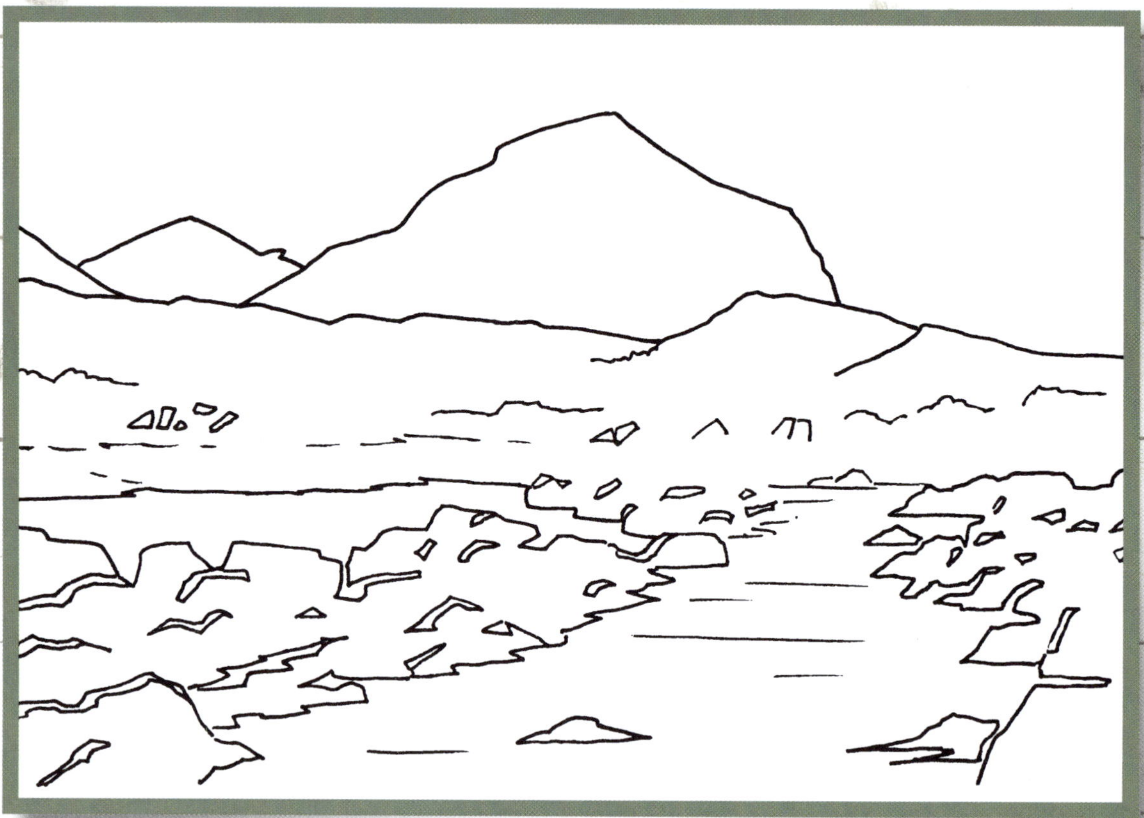

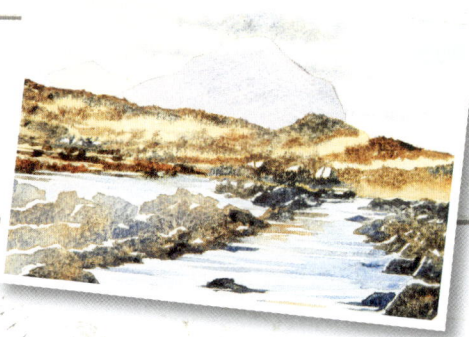

Bright Water 76

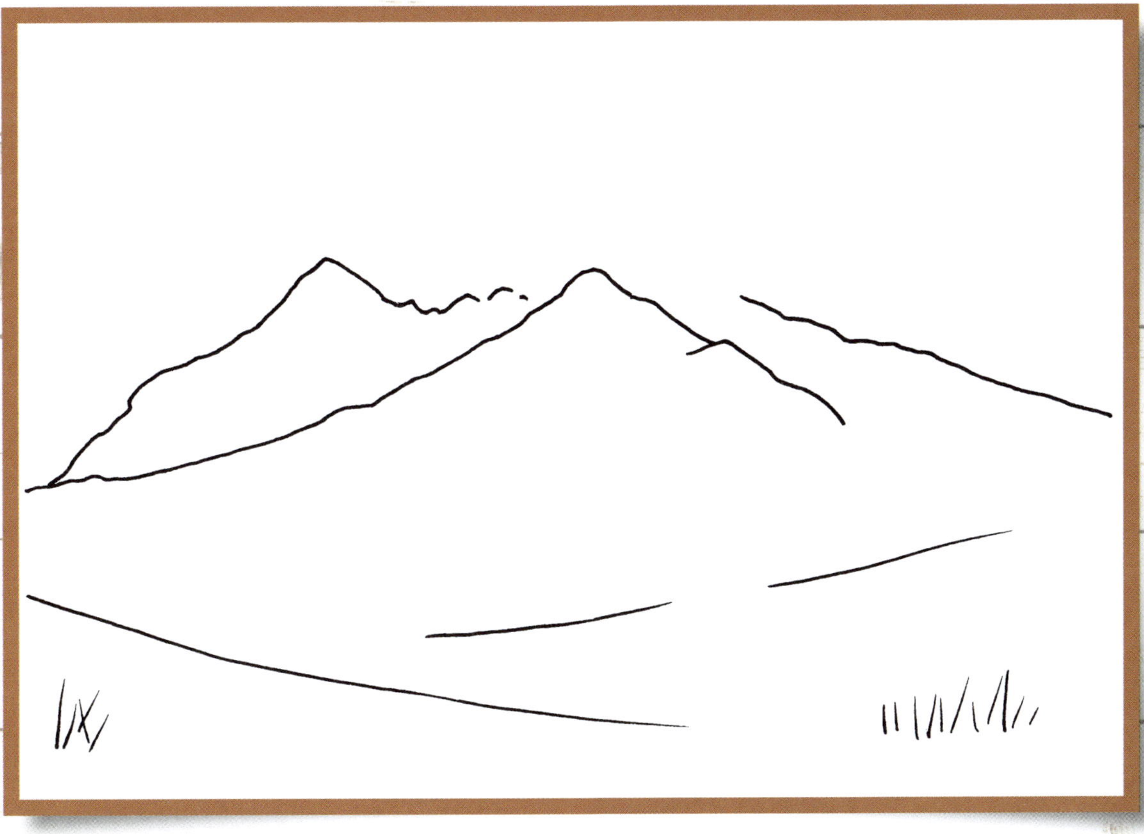

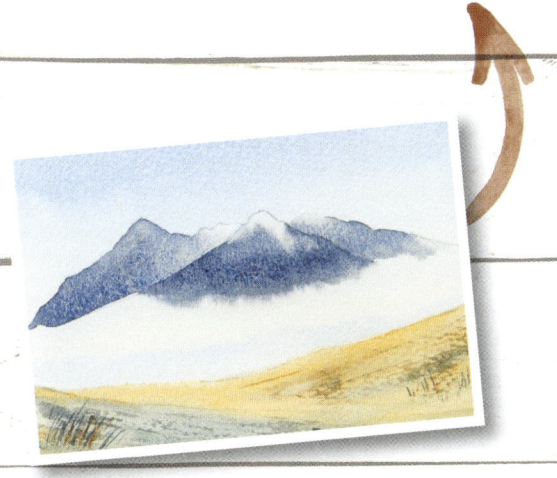

Wreath of mist 80

Index

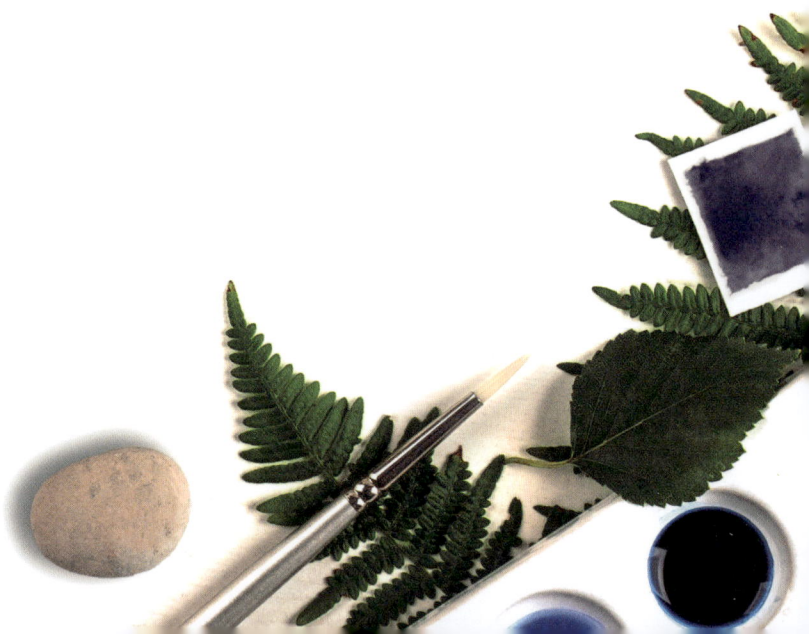